Life Coaching for Teenage Girls

A Practical Guide to Help Achieve Total Empowerment

Justine Cousins

contained within this document, including, but not limited to, errors, omissions, or inaccuracies.

Table of Contents

INTRODUCTION 1

CHAPTER 1: THE POWER OF YOU: SELF-ESTEEM 5

WHY SELF-CONFIDENCE DOESN'T MEAN BEING "OVER-THE-TOP" 5
The Meaning of Self-Esteem: Respect Yourself as You Do Others..................6
The Importance of Self-Esteem: Listen to the Inner Voice 6
What if You're Insecure and Afraid: The Risks of Low Self-Esteem 7
HOW TO RECOVER FROM LOW SELF-ESTEEM...8
Why Everyone Loses Confidence at One Point or Another...........................8
How to Accept Responsibility and Criticism 9
What Not to Accept: Beware of Manipulation! 9
BE YOUR OWN SUPERSTAR: HOW TO BUILD SELF-ESTEEM 11
Tip #1: Explore Your Gifts and Talents 11
Tip #2: Confront Your Weaknesses 11
Tip #3: Ask for Feedback 11
Tip #4: Accept Imperfections...12
Tip #5: Be Kind to Yourself! 12
Tip #6: Set and Work Toward Recovery Goals 12

CHAPTER 2: SOCIAL SKILLS 13

ARE YOU LONELY OR JUST SHY? 13
How You See Yourself vs. How Others See You 14
Making Friends: It's All About Trust, Respect, and Boundaries....................14
WHAT ARE SOCIAL SKILLS AND WHY DO YOU NEED THEM? 15
What Social Skills Are and Why They're NOT About Being Popular.............16
Why You Need Social Skills: Healthy Relationships, Less Drama, More
Support 17
HOW TO BUILD SOCIAL SKILLS...17
Step #1: Practice and Have Fun! 17
Step #2: Start Talking...17
Step #3: Role-Play 18
Step #4: Read the Room...18
Step #5: Listen..19
Step #6: Express Yourself 19
HOW TO FACE AND OVERCOME REJECTION 20
What's Rejection and Why Is Everyone Entitled to It?................................20
Why Being Rejected Isn't Always Bad 20

But…It Hurts! How Do You Accept It Gracefully and Move Forward?.......... 20
When Rejection Is Manipulation/Bullying and What to Do About It 21
SOCIAL MEDIA: WHAT TO AND WHAT NOT TO SHARE 21
Why Social Media Is Great: What to Share.. 21
The Risks of Social Media: The "Fake World" and Made-Up Lifestyles........ 21
What You Don't Want Your Future Employers and Boyfriends to See: What Not to Share 22

CHAPTER 3: PROJECT "YOU": ORGANIZE FOR PERSONAL GROWTH 23

WHAT DOES IT MEAN TO BE ORGANIZED: PREPARE TO SUCCEED 23
Why Should You Always Be Prepared? 24
What Happens When You're Disorganized 25
WHY BEING ORGANIZED IS IMPORTANT FOR HEALTH, SUCCESS, AND HAPPINESS............. 25
Setting Goals, Tasks, and Milestones.. 26
Giving Yourself Enough Time 26
The Magic of Planners, Schedules, and Checklists 27
ORGANIZE YOUR LIFE AND ROUTINES 28
Start Planning!.. 28
Organize Your Room 28
Organize Your School Work 29
Organize Your Time 29
Organize Your Social Life 30
HOW TO STAY ORGANIZED.. 30
Endure for 90 days.. 30
Make It Fun and Creative! 31
Make Organization Into a Ritual 31
Change Your Mind 32
Be Realistic.. 32
Appreciate Your Achievements 32

CHAPTER 4: LOOK INSIDE: WHY MINDFULNESS MATTERS 35

THE WONDERS OF BEING MINDFUL.. 35
What Is Mindfulness? 36
Benefits of Being Mindful 37
HOW TO PRACTICE MINDFULNESS 37
Art and Creativity.. 38
Quiet Contemplation 39
Focused Awareness.. 41
WHAT MINDFULNESS ISN'T: TRAPS TO AVOID 42
The Abuse of Trust: Beware of Predatory Mentors/Scammers.................... 43
Overthinking 44
Escaping Reality.. 44

CHAPTER 5: ACHIEVE AND THRIVE: HOW TO GET MOTIVATED 45

MOTIVATION: WHAT IT MEANS AND WHY IT'S IMPORTANT 45

   The Meaning of Motivation 46

   Why Do You Need Motivation 48

WHAT HAPPENS WHEN YOU'RE NOT MOTIVATED 49

   Drudgery 49

   Failure 49

   Unhappiness 50

   Unfulfilled Achievement 50

HOW TO BOOST MOTIVATION 50

   Visualize Goals 50

   Face Problems 51

   Overcome Fear of Failure 52

   Have a "Contingency Plan" 52

CHAPTER 6: FOCUS 55

FIND YOUR PURPOSE: WHAT IS YOUR "WHY?" 55

   Discover Your Purpose 56

   Live By Your Values 57

   Find Out What Moves You 57

DECLUTTER THE MIND AND GAIN CLARITY 57

   Why Are Your Thoughts Racing? 58

   How to Declutter the Mind 59

   Gain Clarity: Focused Relaxation 59

LAST MINUTE CALL: OVERCOME PROCRASTINATION! 60

   Why Do We Procrastinate? 61

   Why Is Procrastination Bad? 61

   How to Overcome Procrastination 62

CHAPTER 7: EMPOWERMENT: FIND YOUR STRENGTH 65

WHAT PERSONAL POWER IS AND HOW TO EMBRACE IT 65

   Personal Power: The Key to Health and Happiness 66

   Types of Power and How to Gain It 67

HOW TO EMPOWER YOURSELF 68

   Have an (Educated) Opinion 69

   Be Critical 69

   Stand Up for Yourself and Others 70

   Set and Accept Boundaries 71

CHAPTER 8: FEEL GOOD: BE POSITIVE AND RESILIENT 73

WHAT AFFECTS YOUR EMOTIONS 73

   Lifestyle: Diet, Sleep, and Activities 74

   Thoughts and Interactions 74

   Environment 75

   Music and Media 75

How to Limit Negative Thoughts and Experience More Positive Thoughts 76
   Rationalize 76
   Enjoy the Present 77
   Bond 77
   Spend Time Outside 77
How to Channel and Let Go of Negative Feelings 78
   Confide in Loved Ones 78
   Art 78
   Music 79
   Sports 79

CHAPTER 9: WHERE HAPPINESS LIES: HOBBIES AND INTERESTS 81

More Than Quality Time: Why Hobbies and Interests Are Important 81
   Nurturing Talents and Skills 81
   Spending Quality Time With Friends 82
   Building Social Skills 82
Find Out What You're Good At 82
   What Are Your Talents and Strengths? 83
   What Are Your Skills? 83
   What Do You Like to Do? 84
Fun for the Future: How to Use Interests to Advance in Life 84
   Hobbies and Education Choices 85
   Upgrading From Extracurricular Activities to Future Opportunities 86
   Combining Interests to Find Out What You're About 86

CHAPTER 10: OVERCOME FEARS AND ANXIETIES 87

What Is Anxiety? 87
   Meaning 87
   What Does It Look and Feel Like to Be Anxious? 88
   What Causes Anxiety 88
Myths About Anxiety: It's Not ALL Bad 88
How to Cope With Anxiety 90
   How to Calm a Racing Mind 90
   Intrusive Thoughts: What Are They and How Not to Take Them Seriously . 91
   How to "Live in the Present Moment" 92
How to Reduce Anxiety 92
   Reduce Tech and Screen Time 92
   Go to Bed Early—You're Not Missing Out! 93
   Eat Well for a Calm Mind 93
   Journal and Confront Insecurities 94

CHAPTER 11: GIRL STUFF: JUST BETWEEN US! 97

Joys and Hardships of Dating 97
   Are You Ready to Date? 97

Who to Pick: Find Out What You Value 98

Rejection: How to Accept It Gracefully and Recover 98

Stay Safe: How to Protect Yourself 99

UNDERSTAND BOYS 99

What Boys and Girls Have in Common 99

What Makes Boys Different Than Girls 100

How to Have Healthy, Genuine, and Honest Relationships 100

PUBERTY 101

Why Are You Suddenly Different? 101

Changes in Puberty: How Your Body and Mind Develop.....................101

FINAL TIPS FOR GIRLS: FIVE DO'S AND DON'TS 102

Do..102

Don't 103

CONCLUSION **105**

AUTHOR BIO **109**

REFERENCES **111**

Introduction

Do you want to become more confident, sociable, and successful in school? If so, this book provides guidance for every confused teenage girl looking to break free from anxiety and insecurity to become the best version of herself.

In this book, you'll find out:

- **How to overcome insecurities and anxiousness**

Everyone copes with insecurities, from young children to adults. You too are bound to face fears of being unable to do certain things or not being smart, good, or pretty enough. You'll understand where insecurities come from and how to manage them. Have you ever left the house all dressed up and feeling great only to feel yourself diminish and dread the classroom as you approach it? I'll help you understand what anxieties are and how to overcome them by facing fears and learning all about your incredible capabilities. In no time, you'll feel equally amazing no matter where you are or who is there. Hopefully, this will help you learn how to accept fears and insecurities as a natural part of life and master strategies to cope with them without missing out on opportunities to have fun, make friends, learn, and advance in school.

- **How to gain and maintain self-confidence**

By now, you've likely noticed that a large part of what makes some girls more appealing than others is their confidence. You're correct! Low confidence and self-esteem keep many girls from being their best selves and showing all of their qualities. But, what is true confidence? It's not the kind of over-the-top, flashy behavior that only serves to attract attention. Instead, it means to truly believe in yourself and your gifts, even when your capabilities are put to the test and you make a mistake. With this understanding, you'll start enjoying each day and easily overcome difficulties as they arise.

- **How to become more productive and achieve your goals**

Teenage years are the most exciting time in the life of every young woman. After all, you are yet to explore your abilities, find out what you like and want to do, and dedicate hard work to seeing through with commitments that secure your path in the desired direction. If only it was so easy! Most teenagers discover that time seems to slip by them, that they have difficulties with organizing both their time and belongings, and that achieving their goals becomes more difficult once they start to do things.

- **How to use mindfulness to navigate the difficulties of personal, school, and social life**

The things that scare us, hurt us, and drive us all reside within our minds. Past experiences affect how you'll feel and act in future situations, oftentimes in all the wrong ways. You'll find out what mindfulness is and how you can use it to live a fuller life—to find beauty and value even in the most challenging experiences and negative feelings. For this, you'll need to learn how to process difficult feelings and let go to calm yourself and reclaim the sense of inner peace that's so easily broken whenever fights with friends, love problems, or low grades get in the way. Soon, you'll begin to understand how to stay calm and collected even when things aren't going well. Gaining this knowledge will help you find it easier to cope on difficult days and make smart choices.

This short manual will help you understand both yourself and others better. The self-awareness that you'll build through using the advice given in this book will help you understand the connection between what you think and feel and how you interact with others. It helps you understand how other people think as well, which will be the foundation for you to start improving your social skills. You will improve your conversations and relationships. You will better understand what social skills are and why they are important. You'll also learn how to improve social skills to not only have better quality relationships but to also advance in life and education.

You' ll also find out basic information about puberty, dating, and other things that are rarely talked about. This will help you navigate the changes that come with puberty and how to date and socialize while keeping yourself safe. Finally, you'll find out how to spend quality free time by engaging in healthy, creative hobbies and interests. It's important to pursue your creativity and drive and do everything that you can to nurture natural gifts for the sake of a better future. I'll give you a couple of tips and suggestions for how to handle yourself moving forward. Whether you read this book alone or with a parent, you'll get useful instructions that you can begin to apply right after you're finished reading!

Get ready to become more confident, better at making and keeping friends, successful at dating, better at school, and happier with creative endeavors.

Why should you trust Justine Cousins? I have a deep understanding of what it feels like to be a teenage girl, and not only because I went through the trying times of adolescence myself. As a mother of three beautiful daughters, I went through all of the common situations, ups, and downs. I decided not to let my girls go through these experiences alone but instead to get involved. I decided to research and learn and use all the knowledge I gathered to play a proactive role in supporting my daughters in achieving their goals. Not only have I spent a lifetime learning about self-help, but I also dedicated my entire life to showing teenage girls how to enjoy, appreciate, and achieve the best in life. Do you want to become one of these girls? Do you want to break free from standards imposed by your social circle, social media, and mainstream platforms to discover your true values, talents, and skills? If so, start with Chapter 1 and learn all about what self-esteem is and how you can start feeling better about yourself TODAY!

Chapter 1:

The Power of YOU: Self-Esteem

Why Self-Confidence Doesn't Mean Being "Over-The-Top"

Every teenage girl wants to be unique. Attention feels good for all teenagers, and there's nothing wrong with that. However, young people often do wrong things to attract attention. Sometimes, these things can be harmful for them and others, and other times, they are producing the opposite effect than intended. Have you ever seen someone acting "over-the-top" in an effort to be popular? Do you think that it looks good and achieves the desired result? More importantly, do you think that person feels good or they're only pretending in front of others?

Many people, including teenagers, choose to act dramatic or try to stand out at all costs. Sometimes, it's someone's loud speech, laughing, and in-your-face jokes and mannerisms. Other times, it's the way of clothing and wearing hair and make-up that cause the person to stand out. Being over-the-top isn't the only or the best way to have people's attention. In fact, nurturing your true self-confidence is the only way to present yourself in a positive way that won't only make people look at you but also remember and respect you. But, for that, it's first necessary that you respect and appreciate yourself.

The Meaning of Self-Esteem: Respect Yourself as You Do Others

It's sad to say, but most teenagers, as well as adults who—don't forget—used to be teens, don't realize the wonderful traits that they have: the smarts, the beauty, the innate worthiness of love, respect, and good things in life. The word "self-esteem" describes a profound sense of inner worthiness. That worthiness applies to everything—kindness, love, respect, success, and happiness. Yet, so many people struggle with self-esteem. This might come as a surprise, but most people's self-esteem is put to the test throughout life. Looking from outside, a person might appear good looking, have a committed boyfriend or girlfriend, plenty of money to dress and travel, and a really cool job. But, most people struggle—just like you.

What do you appreciate about your friends and family? What are the qualities that make you admire them and want them by your side? Think about the way you look at yourself in comparison to the traits you like in others. Do you think of yourself as "less than" other people in some way? The great news is that the traits that we like about other people are the traits that we actually possess, no matter how difficult it is to understand that sometimes.

The Importance of Self-Esteem: Listen to the Inner Voice

It's hard to describe self-esteem because you can't picture it, measure it with a test, or screen for it in a lab. It doesn't come in a bottle— although it would be amazing if it did. Instead, it is a deep inner voice that tells you that you're worthy of good things and above wrongful behaviors. Have you ever caught yourself saying, "I won't put up with this" or "You can't do this to me" when someone mistreated you? A lot of the time, it's hard to stand up for yourself for many reasons. You're not sure if you're right, and you don't want to pick a fight. Yet, despite all that, something inside won't let you "put up" with things that you know you shouldn't. Likewise, you sometimes know that certain behaviors and actions are beneath you. If you've ever said, "I won't say/do that, that's not who I am!" then you know the feeling of being coerced or pressured into saying or doing something you know to be wrong. Although persisting with your selected moral values and restrictions give teenagers a feeling of "being right," more often than not, the pressure to fit in is too much to handle.

What if You're Insecure and Afraid: The Risks of Low Self-Esteem

While the good news is that everyone has a self-esteem that can be built up, the bad news is that it can also be hurt. When someone's self-esteem is hurt, they feel humiliated, unworthy, and profoundly unloved and rejected. Have you ever felt that way? If so, in which situations? Most people, no matter their age, feel hurt and ashamed when they fail at something, when they're criticized, or when they feel verbally and emotionally attacked. Those are the experiences that most children, teenagers, and adults face. While they do contribute to insecurities and anxiousness, injuries to self-esteem like these are very easy to heal from. However, when criticism becomes abuse, and conflict turns out to be violence, abuse, or manipulation, the hurt "runs deeper." It's much harder to recover from because most people aren't able to even recognize that their self-esteem is hurt. In this case, damaged self-esteem becomes anger, depression, or extreme anxiousness that prevents young girls from processing their experience, healing, and moving on.

To some degree, young girls like yourself benefit from a tolerable, non-abusive dose of negative feedback. It teaches you to think very rationally about things that are being said to you and decide for yourself whether the criticism "holds merit." However, when negative feedback and relationships aren't being processed well, like when you don't want to talk about your insecurities, you might become too insecure to the point of reaching anxiety or depression. Similarly, trauma can very easily lead to problems with mood, like anxiety and depression, or even behavior, in the form of anger and aggressiveness—depending on the severity of the emotional injury.

The severity of injury to one's self-esteem doesn't necessarily depend on the traumatic experience, although there is a strong connection. An injury to self-esteem is a form of hurtful belief that a person deserved whatever happened to them because they're bad, flawed, unlovable, or many other labels that they attach to themselves along the way.

While more extreme risks from damaged self-esteem include mental health issues, substance abuse, and problematic/risky behaviors, there are also effects that are harder to spot. When a person has damaged self-esteem, they are profoundly insecure. After all, they believe in the worst about themselves. Such insecurities can lead to problems in friendships and in school. Sometimes, girls who have low self-esteem are willing to do wrong things to get others' attention and approval at the expense of their health and well-being.

How to Recover From Low Self-Esteem

Why Everyone Loses Confidence at One Point or Another

Most people have fragile self-esteem. Unless they learn how to think about their self-image and do conscious things to improve self-esteem, almost everyone experiences low self-esteem at some point in their life. This is because self-esteem is made from things that we believe about ourselves, and these beliefs can change based on our experiences and the people around us. For example, if you're surrounded by good people who want you to be happy and succeed, they will be supportive, forgiving, and more considerate of your feelings. However, when you're around people who don't wish you well, their words and actions are done with the purpose of causing harm. Yet, it's not always possible to choose your company or to only be around good people who wish you well. Both teenagers and adults spend major parts of their day in settings like schools and work, where there's at least one person who dislikes us. It doesn't matter whether or not the dislike is justified; having to spend a lot of time next to people who aren't well-intentioned takes a toll on a person's self-esteem. That's why the majority of people know someone who they don't get along with or have difficult memories about how some people berated or hurt them. While it's not always possible to preserve self-esteem, it's always possible to work on improving it!

How to Accept Responsibility and Criticism

Are people right when they say something bad or hurtful? This is the most difficult question to answer and confront and the most frequent reason why girls don't choose to face low self-esteem. In that sense, having a set of reasonable criteria for answering that question is a good way to start. However, your self-esteem shouldn't depend on whether or not you find certain criticism to be accurate. Instead, your sense of self should be resilient to any injury with the ability to accept responsibility and criticism.

Most of the time, self-esteem suffers when someone points out that we have a negative trait or that we said or did something bad, but there are also situations when words are said with a clear intention of hurting and without any desire for a healthy, constructive conversation. The first type of negative feedback often makes girls feel too ashamed to even think whether or not it's accurate—and that's the biggest problem. Having the courage to think about the accuracy of the remark usually helps relieve anxiety surrounding it. Understanding the accuracy of the negative feedback usually shows what you can change for the better, while its inaccuracy usually means that the person who said something bad to you either did it just to hurt you or was simply wrong. The similar approach is good whenever someone insults or teases you. If you know that the person is coming from a bad place, then there's no reason to give significance to their words. However, if you feel hurt because you're afraid that they're right, you should talk to people you trust and try to rationalize the entire incident.

Addressing behaviors is more straightforward. When people criticize something you did, there are common rules and boundaries that can serve as a reference. If a person's criticism of your behavior aligns with common rules and norms, you should accept it and commit to doing better in the future.

What Not to Accept: Beware of Manipulation!

Classmates, relatives, and boyfriends sometimes truly don't have our best interests at heart when giving feedback. Instead, the words that they say reflect the need to either hurt you on purpose or get you to say or act in a way you otherwise wouldn't that benefits them. This is called manipulation. Sometimes, people want to have more control or power over another person and their actions. For example, if a friend or boyfriend fears that you might leave them, they can start criticizing your intellect or appearance. The intention behind putting you down is for you to feel like you need that person more than you actually do. Or, if you're not close with the manipulator, the goal is for them to obtain some sort of gain on your expense, even if it's only to stand out as being stronger, cooler, and more powerful.

The reason why manipulators are so hard to deal with is that they act friendly when they need you to trust them and only say hurtful things when it benefits them—irrelevant of real necessity or reasoning to have a conversation.

Recognizing manipulation isn't as difficult as not letting it get to you. Since manipulators distance themselves from people who are resistant to their words, showing that you're not "buying" into the manipulation should suffice. When someone is saying hurtful things, ask yourself these questions:

- Are they qualified? Do they know enough to make the claims that they are making?
- Is there actual reasoning or justification for them to bring up the things they do? Do their words bring real good or improvement to someone, or do they benefit only the manipulator?

The final answers tell you whether or not to believe that any criticism or accusations are true. The more you practice this form of reasoning, the better you preserve your self-esteem (Eva, 2018).

Be Your Own Superstar: How to Build Self-Esteem

Tip #1: Explore Your Gifts and Talents

If believing the best things about yourself requires persuasion, finding out about your skills and talents is a good way to start. Write down all of the amazing things that you can do and any hobbies, crafts, or chores that you're talented for.

Tip #2: Confront Your Weaknesses

Most people believe that admitting their weaknesses is something awful, but it's not. Some people are always late, and others snap easily or argue when they know they're wrong just to save face. Some people are natural-born artists but don't do well with sports, while for others, jumping off of a plane with a parachute is a joke compared to cooking. Confronting your weaknesses or things that you're not very good at gives you the advantage of choosing whether you want to make peace with your weakness or change it and learn something new.

Tip #3: Ask for Feedback

People with low self-esteem usually have issues with school, relationships, and/or behavior. Whether you're just shy or you used to get into fights, it's great to hear people's honest opinions of you. Hearing about your traits that people like and dislike gives you an upper hand when talking to classmates and new people. It also helps you understand that you, like all other people, are a complex personality with good and bad sides.

Tip #4: Accept Imperfections

While us girls enjoy thinking about our positive sides, the negatives, or perceived negatives, often bug and upset us. No one is perfect, and neither are you. Accepting that there are certain things about yourself that you don't like but can't change is the first step toward loving yourself unconditionally—good qualities and imperfections included!

Tip #5: Be Kind to Yourself!

Reminding yourself about positive traits and the things you like, whether it's your appearance or personality, improves your self-esteem.

Tip #6: Set and Work Toward Recovery Goals

Set goals for improving your self-esteem, like

- Standing up for yourself when someone is treating you unfairly.
- Not giving in to other people's requests when you don't want to.
- Only hanging out with people who appreciate and respect you.
- Not doing wrong things so that others will like or fear you.
- Etc.

Once you break down specific goals with building up your self-esteem, they will consistently remind you of the direction in which you're going and the changes that you want to make.

Chapter 2:

Social Skills

Are You Lonely or Just Shy?

All teenagers have insecurities and feel like they don't belong at one point or another. You might have a handful of friends you've known your whole life that make you feel truly comfortable, but the rest of the time, you feel intensely self-conscious. Am I right? Some of the insecurities that come to light when you least need them—in class, when you're supposed to be having fun with friends, or when you're talking to a crush—might sound like: Does my hair look good? Is my make-up still in place? Are my thighs/belly too large?

To some degree, we've all been there! Only, some girls hide their insecurities well thanks to their social skills. Although they are as self-conscious as you are, they still manage to smile, keep their back straight when they walk, make jokes, listen, and communicate to other people throughout the day. Yet, there are also those who prefer to keep to themselves. There's nothing wrong with some 'alone' time, but when a girl feels unable to bond with other girls, that's a bit more than just being shy.

Being self-conscious about how you look, talk, and come across to others is an everyday experience, but when it starts to bug you, keep you from making friends, and getting good grades, that means it's time for a change.

How You See Yourself vs. How Others See You

The rule of thumb for adolescence is that you always see yourself more negatively than others do. When you're sitting in a classroom or you're going out with a group of friends, shyness can make you feel terrible about yourself when there's actually nothing wrong with your appearance or behavior. For example, you might imagine yourself to be frizzy, with smudged make-up and poorly fitted clothes, while others have no clue what style you were going for. They might even like your grungy look, and compared to the rest of the polished girls, you might come across as more chill and laid back. That's not bad! But, your attitude plays a much bigger role in how others will see you.

If building social skills seems like science fiction, just keep in mind that these skills are a lot more about how you choose to present yourself than they are about who you truly are. Remember this distinction, because it's crucial in making friends and overcoming shyness. Socializing is a taught skill, and in the following sections, you too will learn how to do it!

Making Friends: It's All About Trust, Respect, and Boundaries

How much do you love your closest friends? Are they like family to you? Perhaps, you'd like to make more friends, but you're afraid that they might distract you from old ones. Or, you have only one or two friends, and those relationships aren't that great either. Solitude, in itself, is not a flaw. You're not a 'freak' or a 'loner' if you struggle with making friends. But, perhaps you lack a couple of crucial pieces of information to do better.

First, understand that friends match by their interests, temper, and sensibility. When people are alike, they understand each other and are better able to trust one another. Trust is a crucial part of friendship, and demonstrating that you're a trustworthy person will make you more appealing.

Respect is the second element of a healthy friendship. To respect others means to treat them with dignity, grace, and consideration. These terms might sound "old school," but in real life, being respectful of yourself and others will get you far in life.

Being kind and respectful doesn't mean that you should let anyone mistreat you, and that's where boundaries come in as a much cooler, modern element. Standing up for yourself and not allowing anyone to disrespect or mistreat you commands others' respect and makes a person more appealing.

The "Best Friends Forever (BFF) Myth:" Truths About Friendship That No One Will Tell You

True friendships are never perfect, but they are honest and committed. Most of us, when we were your age, thought that a girl's best friend is always there for her and that they never fight. The group is either big or small, but they're all flawless and never hurt one another. This isn't true in real life. Stable friendships are just like those that you have with family: You see each others' qualities and flaws, you make mistakes and overcome challenges, and you have fights and move on. The sooner you give up on an expectation to have a perfect BFF, the happier you'll be!

What Are Social Skills and Why Do You Need Them?

Have you ever wondered why some girls have the appeal, a sort of memorable presence, and a charisma that makes everyone like them? If you've noticed, this charisma may not always mean that a girl is prettier or smarter than the rest of her group, but there's something inviting about her that makes most people want to be her friend. The secret to personal likeability lies in social skills.

What Social Skills Are and Why They're NOT About Being Popular

Social know-how is a set of skills in

- Talking: Being interactive, or communicative, isn't just about talking a lot. It is in knowing how to engage and understand how another person feels about a certain topic and about the conversation. It's also about knowing the right tone and style to use with different people while staying true to yourself and the way you wish to represent yourself.
- Listening and observing: Likable people listen and observe. That way, they learn details about others, such as their likes and dislikes, mood, interests, style choices, and living philosophies. You don't have to change or adapt based on what you observe; instead, keep the knowledge in mind when approaching others.
- Manners: Body language and non-verbal cues can attract or deter people. Sitting and standing straight with your head high, shoulders relaxed, and hands laid down confidently next to your hips is considered the right way to go. This sort of stance appeals to most styles and age groups, and it has a subtle impact on people that make them want to be around that person. It's called 'inviting' in one word.
- Personal Representation: How you carry yourself dictates how others will see you, no matter how insensitive that might sound. If you are dressed properly for the occasion, in clean clothes that fit, you're more likely to get noticed (in a good way) than if you overdress. Teenage girls tend to go over-the-top with outfits, which often causes the opposite effect than what was intended.

Avoid the 'Like Me' Syndrome and Be Authentic

Instead of wanting others to like you, be "your own biggest fan" and engage with people out of curiosity or a desire to bond, help, or have fun. When girls want to be likable too much, they not only go overboard with clothes and makeup, but they also allow people to mistreat them, say they agree with things when they don't, and succumb to peer pressure. You don't want to be the girl who sells her authenticity for a couple of likes!

Why You Need Social Skills: Healthy Relationships, Less Drama, More Support

To build social skills, you first need to adopt a bit of a more cool-headed approach to relationships. Understand that learning social skills is as technical as learning how to use a computer program or a new app. There are clear rules and methods that you can use to add quality to your relationships. With good social skills, you'll get into fewer fights because you'll know how to understand others and compromise. Building social skills will help you find a dependable group of friends and teachers who will be there to support your growth.

How to Build Social Skills

There are several simple ways to start building social skills:

Step #1: Practice and Have Fun!

Social skills are all about gaining knowledge through fun, spontaneous experiences. In that sense, they're more about small talk and light chats than deep, complex conversations. Small talk can be awkward, particularly for young girls. But, it's necessary to "break the ice" and overcome nervousness.

Step #2: Start Talking

Saying anything relevant to the situation or the topic, even if only confirming what others are saying and nodding your head, is better than staying silent and keeping your thoughts to yourself. If you don't like drawing too much attention to yourself, or you don't feel particularly opinionated about the topic, expressing acknowledgment will suffice. However, keep in mind to use every opportunity to share your opinions, not only when asked. Do this in a way that's appropriate for the situation and the group using the following tips:

- Sense the tone and the group dynamic of the conversation and match it with your behavior and words (e.g. whether the situation is formal or informal, fun or serious, intimate or more distanced).
- Don't have an agenda when talking to others—be genuine. If you approach a group with the goal of getting attention, you might say or do things that look cringy or out-of-place.
- Compliment others in suitable ways. You can point out that someone's look was particularly nice that day or that their essay was great. Keep in mind that people who don't know you very well won't appreciate too many compliments, particularly if they're about appearance or personal traits—it might come across as intrusive.

Step #3: Role-Play

Do you struggle to keep up a conversation? Then practice! Have a fun girls night with a couple of your besties or go out for lunch or dinner with a parent or a cousin. Pretend that you're in different situations. For example, re-enact meetings with your classmates before class and during breaks, talking to teachers, giving presentations, etc.

Step #4: Read the Room

Understanding the tone of the social situation and everyone involved is crucial for social skills. You want to avoid cracking jokes when everyone else is having a serious discussion or getting too fired up about the topic when everyone else seems to joke about it. Things like these look out of place and inconsiderate.

Step #5: Listen

Have you ever wondered what truly makes someone noticeable and popular? It's not about being flashy, loud, and flirtatious, wearing the outfit that's "most in," or having the most expensive gadgets. It's about having people consider you important to them. How do you become important to new people? You do this by listening and understanding what they're about, sharing what interests them, and helping solve whatever bugs them (a.k.a. problems). This isn't the same as giving unwanted advice or "meddling" in people's private business. It's about responding to what people say to you—and only what's said directly to you—with genuine care and within the real boundaries of your relationship. It is a gentle balance in deciding what to say and what to keep to yourself, and exercises will help you find that balance.

Step #6: Express Yourself

Finally, let others learn more about you. There are things that are safe and appropriate to share with everyone, like your interests, hobbies, and activities. You can talk about these things as much as you'd like, given that the other person looks interested and engages in the conversation. Topics like beliefs, family, religion, social attitudes, or personal issues and problems can make or break relationships. Share too much and you expose yourself to ridicule and manipulation, while being too closed can make people feel like you're hiding something from them and isolating yourself. The golden rule is to share as much as the other person shares, while keeping in mind that they can't be expected to keep things confidential. Don't trust everyone when they say that they'll keep a secret to themselves—as they usually don't—and only share information that's okay for everyone to know.

How to Face and Overcome Rejection

What's Rejection and Why Is Everyone Entitled to It?

As a teenager, you likely dread being rejected more than anything else. You're afraid that your crush will say 'No' or that you'll approach someone to make small talk and they'll simply ignore you. As much as I'd like to say that these fears are exaggerated, they're not. In fact, people learn to appreciate anyone willing to be their friend only after they turn 20 and experience loneliness enough times. Rejection is painful, and it's a reality of adolescence. The best and only way to overcome it is to accept it as it is. Everyone is entitled to turn down a person and decide that they don't want to talk to or date someone—including you.

Why Being Rejected Isn't Always Bad

People's rejection shows you what type of behavior is considered unwanted, although that doesn't justify the unnecessary cruelty or mockery that often comes with it. When you approach someone and get shut down, you simply know who to not to count on or pay attention to. It's alright for people not to want to hang out with you as long as it doesn't cross into bullying and you have enough friends for a satisfying social life.

But…It Hurts! How Do You Accept It Gracefully and Move Forward?

Accepting rejection without trying to force someone to change their mind, and doing so respectfully, shows grace and elegance. If you approach someone to say "Hi" and they just ignore you, that means that they have poor manners—not you. Simply smile and walk away without making a big deal out of it. Remind yourself that it's their loss, not yours.

When Rejection Is Manipulation/Bullying and What to Do About It

Although everyone has a right to refuse to talk to or socialize with someone and the duty to accept rejection, there is a point where rejection becomes bullying. When it's organized within a group or a class, with a clear intention to hurt your feelings, you should report it. Similarly, rejection that serves to humiliate or get you to do something that another person wants is manipulative. The person counts on you wanting to do whatever they want you to to get back in their good graces. Don't let them have that, and instead, accept their rejection and move on.

Social Media: What TO and What NOT to Share

Why Social Media Is Great: What to Share

Social media is great to share fun times with friends, your hobbies and interests, as well as causes that you support. It's fun, and it gives you opportunities to exchange messages and opinions. It enables you to contact friends and distant relatives as well as connect with communities and organizations that you like and support.

The Risks of Social Media: The "Fake World" and Made-Up Lifestyles

However, social media also has a dark side. It can become maliciously critical and abusive, and it can also give you a false idea about how others' lives look. All of this, combined, can make you feel insecure. There's also the risk from bullying, an organized effort by an individual or a group to send offensive and threatening messages or insult/slander someone on social media. The best way to cope with bullying is to report it!

What You Don't Want Your Future Employers and Boyfriends to See: What Not to Share

Although the same rules and laws apply to social media as everywhere else, it's almost impossible to impose them or keep track of people's identities. Because of this, you never know who can download your content and use it against you in some way. Images, posts, and comments that are offensive and inappropriate for your age can potentially harm your future. They are free for anyone to access, despite your privacy settings. Remember to share only age-appropriate content that can't be misinterpreted or used against you in the future.

Chapter 3:

Project "YOU": Organize for Personal Growth

Success and happiness come from many things. Having trusting, healthy relationships, doing well at school, staying healthy, and creating opportunities for yourself are the highlights of a teen girl's everyday life. However, all of these things have one thing in common: They require you to have an organized, orderly, and structured life.

What Does It Mean to Be Organized: Prepare to Succeed

Being organized means living a purposeful life that's geared towards a goal. The word "goal" might sound a bit cold or dry, like something found only in firms and crammy offices. However, goals apply to all areas of life. Being healthy, having a fun social life, having strong and healthy relationships, having good grades, moving toward your desired future—all of these are goals, and they revolve around fulfilling your desires. Your days might pass in trying to keep up with school, finding the most time to have fun and socialize as possible, and pursuing crushes, but is that a purposeful life? If all of the things you do are accidental, spontaneous, and unplanned, it's possible that you feel a bit lost and overwhelmed. If you don't organize well, your date can overlap with revising for tomorrow's test, or you might have to choose between meeting your friends or going out with your family.

Organization can remove a lot of tension and rush from your life. To organize means to plan your life by areas, keeping lists of tasks and chores and, of course, thinking about the things you want to achieve (goals) and the best ways to do that.

Why Should You Always Be Prepared?

Keeping your closet neat, your planner up-to-date, your stomach fed, and your body clean ensures a stress-free morning. Doing homework right after you get back from school, instead of waiting for the due date, relieves the concern of failing while freeing up more time for you in the coming days. Laying out your outfit the night before ensures that you'll get ready easily and wear the most comfortable outfit for the day. Preparation sets you up for success and helps you feel confident and secure. You are still learning about taking up responsibilities, and without preparation, these responsibilities can feel like too much. You might feel incapable of doing things that you're perfectly capable of doing simply because you didn't give yourself enough time to plan or try things beforehand. Preparation helps you reach full potential, whether it's with school, friends, or work.

For example, when you make plans with your friends, you're more likely to have a good time if you figure out where to go and what to do. If you just agree where to meet to hang out, it's possible to get bored or even end up arguing if all of you want to do different things. Instead, if you all meet up to plan your day or evening out beforehand, everyone has an opportunity to say what they'd like to do, and there's enough time to agree and compromise.

Preparation also gives you an opportunity to predict obstacles and figure out a "Plan B," or what to do in case something goes wrong. What to do if you get nervous during exams and how to calm down, where to go with your crew if your favorite spot is closed, or it starts to rain during a beach day—all of these are common issues that happen in real life. Timely preparation and planning helps anticipate possible complications and figure out what to do if they occur.

What Happens When You're Disorganized

Failing to organize can cause a lot of heartache, including

- Failure: When your assignment and test schedule is out of control, you can end up with bad grades no matter how talented, smart, or hard working you are.
- Stress: Not knowing what to do next, trying to do multiple things at once, fearing that you'll forget to do something, and getting up knowing that you won't be able to get everything done by the end of the day is so stressful and frustrating!
- Conflict: Without a goal, a plan, and preparation, you can easily get into conflict with anyone who crosses your path. From a sibling rushing you to get out of the bathroom, a parent who notices that you're running late, and friends who can't "get on the same page"—everyone argues when a situation is chaotic.
- Insecurity: Not knowing where you're headed in life, what comes next, and how best to do it can make you doubt your talents and capacities. Not having enough time to get ready can make you feel bad about your looks, and being unprepared for class can make you doubt your abilities.
- Anxiousness: When your life becomes chaotic, you're constantly arguing with friends and family, you can't get anything done on time, and you doubt your abilities, you're bound to start feeling anxious.

Why Being Organized Is Important for Health, Success, and Happiness

Organization gives you direction, a sense of control, readiness, and confidence. From getting up in the morning, going to school, meeting friends, and going for interviews, organization empowers you to be your best self. It also allows everyone to see your biggest strengths and best sides. It will enable you to look and do the best you can while preventing failure, problems, and conflicts.

Setting Goals, Tasks, and Milestones

Planning starts from formulating one goal that's later broken down into several goals, areas of life, milestones, and tasks. That way, every little thing that you do throughout the day brings you closer to what you want in life. For example, your general goal might be to live a fulfilling life. Living a fulfilling life means being happy, healthy, and successful, which can be your specific goals. Then, you can think about how these goals reflect on different areas of your life. Happiness is obtained through health, relationships, and activities, and the same goes for health and success. Now, your general goal is being broken up into specific goals that you can formulate in simple sentences (e.g. "I want to have a healthy diet, train, and check my health regularly"). After you formulate each of the specific goals, you can break it down into milestones. For example, success can be broken down into achieving a specific grade level that you want for a further academic path or employment, winning competitions related to your hobbies and interests, or finding a targeted number of people that make you feel confident, safe, and accepted. Then, you can break down each of these specific milestones into tasks. For example, having good grades will require keeping up with school and homework, paying attention to your learning schedule, etc. while making friends will require time to think about who would be a good match for you, visiting new places, arranging time to hang out, etc. Once you break down all of your goals into tasks this way, they become a lot more manageable, realistic, and achievable.

Giving Yourself Enough Time

Once you break down your goals into tasks, start thinking about each of them and the best way to complete them. Think about how much time it will take, what sort of tools, accessories, and help you'll need, how much money it will take, who you need to consult, what obstacles you can expect to face, etc. Take enough time to think about each general and specific goal and the best ways that they can be achieved in your daily life. The same goes for milestones and tasks. What you need to do to achieve what you want depends not only on your capabilities and interests but also on your family's ability to support you.

Taking enough time to plan your life and think about what you want, whether it's making sure that you're safe when you go out or that you get a scholarship for a prominent college, will leave enough time for you to think about different options. Girls whose families face economic struggles often feel like they have fewer possibilities, but that doesn't have to be true. If you want to achieve something, but you don't feel like the resources for it are available, you can take the time and search for organizations and communities that provide the needed support. There are many ways to overcome limitations. Many girls discover the opportunities that were available once it's too late, and they make decisions and commitments that are hard to get back from. Don't let this happen, and seek everything life has to give before giving up!

The Magic of Planners, Schedules, and Checklists

Now that you likely have numerous amazing ideas for a masterplan for a fabulous life, you might notice that keeping all of those goals and tasks in your head is just too much! How long before you start forgetting to do things or you get tangled in all of the ideas and to-do's? Without a planner, a schedule, and daily, weekly, and monthly checklists, your life can easily become chaotic again. Planners are a must for every striving teen who wants to make the best of her life. They allow you to make different schedules, and note and mark weeks, days, and even hours in a day by what you want to do and how you want to do it. Schedules are then entered into planners for a more specific guide for what to do and when to do it. Classes, meetings, dates, training, hobbies, crafts, and free time all consist of activities. These activities have a certain order, timing, and things that you need to prepare and bring with you. When you enter all of your schedules into your planner, you will get a clear overview of what your day will look like. You'll know exactly what to do and how to get ready. You won't forget anything, miss out on appointments, or feel overwhelmed.

Organize Your Life and Routines

However, organization doesn't end with making plans and schedules. It is a wholesome approach to life that will require you to get your space, work, and social life in order for best results. Following through with plans and commitments will be truly difficult if you can't find your things or need ages to create an outfit. In this sense, organizing your life will take insight into all of the areas to find a time and place for each item. When all of your things are in place, it will be a lot easier to go about your days. You'll feel much more prepared and empowered.

Start Planning!

After getting your planner and filling in your goals, milestones, and schedules, turn to your personal life. Your items, belongings, papers, and appointments are going to have to be properly arranged to get the same sense of control, clarity, and organization that comes with making plans and schedules. Talk to your parents or caregivers about getting folders, stickers, label makers, boxes, containers, and other organizers that might help arrange all of your items for quick and easy access.

Organize Your Room

Girls' rooms are famously colorful, but also notoriously messy. Are your clothes scattered all over the room with mismatched socks piled up in your drawers and shoes peeking underneath the bed? I'm not questioning your cleanliness, just the knowledge and habit of keeping your room orderly. Being messy can sometimes feel fun because it's rebellious. It might give you a feeling that you're living by your rules and escaping the drudgery of everyday life. But, it's not like that. Organizing your room will make it feel more comfortable and fun to be in, and you'll do it by arranging all of your items in the following order:

- Type and station: All similar items should be placed in a single station, closet, drawer, etc.

- Purpose: Then, you can sort items using a logical system of their use. For example, if you're arranging your makeup, keep foundations closer to the top or the front of your make-up drawer and your mascara and setting spray toward the back. That way, you'll get to pull out items in the same order in which you use them.
- Color and size: Clothes, hobby supplies, hair supplies, jewelry, shoes, and accessories can be color and size-coded, whenever these features are highly relevant.
- Labeling: If you're struggling to remember where each of the items belongs, you can apply labels or stickers with the item category written out.

Organize Your School Work

Similar rules apply to school. Get thicker, larger folders in different colors and designs for each subject, and then two smaller folders that can fit into the larger ones for each subject. Write out [Subject-School/Homework] on each folder, and then pack the smaller folders into the bigger ones. That way, all of your assignments and notes will stay sorted. You won't worry about stacking homework in a bag and losing it somewhere along the way.

Organize Your Time

Planners usually come with a timetable, but your scheduling doesn't end there. You also need to enter monthly, weekly, and daily reminders for when to start getting ready for a task, as well as when a particular task item starts and finishes. You can create reminders on your phone and laptop and rely on timely pings to let you know when it's time to take a shower, snack, revise, do math, call your BFF, or get a gift for your cousin's birthday. Have you ever caught yourself wishing that someone reminded you to do a couple of small tasks that would make your entire day better? Reminders can give you just that!

Organize Your Social Life

The same principles apply to your social life, only there are a couple more things to consider. Meeting your friends and going out isn't only about showing up on time. It also takes time to choose an outfit, get ready, shower, shave, moisturize, do your hair and makeup, etc. Social occasions sometimes require calling in to make and confirm reservations, buy clothing and shoes, arrange transportation, etc. If only one of these elements is out of place, the entire event can ruin you! Keeping a separate social calendar isn't only a privilege of rich adults. It's a great, fun way to pay attention to your socializing habits and improve them wherever possible.

How to Stay Organized

Getting organized isn't difficult, but staying that way is. Your journey begins with buying nice-looking supplies, like planners, stickers, markers, boxes, and labels. It continues by thinking about all the wonderful things that you want and the real ways to get it. The process might last a week or two, and I promise you'll have an amazing time. But, as true as it is for an adult, it is for a young girl—things are easier said than done. You'll get a lot better right upon gaining perspective of your life, but putting everything you planned in motion and following through is a major commitment and a responsibility that won't always feel easy, pretty, or fun. Here's how to stay organized and committed to your goals:

Endure for 90 days

Following through with your life plan will require new habits. Except, gaining new habits isn't easy. In fact, for adults, it's SO difficult that they actually pay people to train them and monitor their progress! Luckily, you're at a golden age where it's (somewhat) easy to make changes. Still, a habit isn't "done" until you begin to do it without having to put in effort. Whether it's getting up on time in the morning or laying out your outfit in the evening, you've completely made a habit out of useful things once you catch yourself doing it spontaneously, like brushing teeth in the morning or putting your shoes on before leaving home.

Make It Fun and Creative!

While some of your issues truly are big and significant, the good news is that organizing, planning, and engaging in personal growth is the best thing you can do for yourself (and everyone else) right now. Your family and teachers do a rough 90% of the things they do to see you well and happy, so getting the best out of it—and having the time of your life in the process—is everything that everyone who cares about you wants you to do. Don't think of personal growth as a chore, but instead, setting the stage for a happy, healthy life.

Make Organization Into a Ritual

Did you know that there are dozens of planning brands and communities that engage with teenagers around visualizing, planning, and creating ideas to fulfill their dreams. There are specialized Etsy shops that sell gorgeous planners, stickers, and accessories so that planning becomes a true pleasure. With that in mind, inspired organization can be truly enjoyable, especially if you incorporate it into morning and evening rituals. For example, you can have a cup of tea while reviewing your planner and writing your task list or sorting your shoes while giving yourself a facial. In the evening, you can play some music or your favorite TV show while writing in your journal, congratulating yourself on things that you achieved that day and planning what to do tomorrow. That way, when setbacks and challenges arise, you'll have dozens more useful habits as a tool that make you happy to figure out ways to overcome them.

Change Your Mind

It's OK to alter, add, or completely scrap some items from your plan. In fact, learning to do that right now will save you from changing into a hard-headed adult who won't admit that something's just not working out. The same way you're supposed to accept rejection (mentioned in the previous chapter), it's alright to give up on ideas or plans that prove too much or don't seem to serve your goal the way you thought they will. For example, if you wanted to take up a new hobby, you might get stuck at a beginner stage for months, while the rest of your group advances to the intermediate level. A skill learned is always a useful one, but you don't have to persist with the activity if you feel like it's not giving you what you anticipated it would—either enjoyment or potential credits for long-term success.

Be Realistic

You can imagine and put everything you want on paper, but some things likely won't work out. Perhaps, you had a different idea about how certain things and accomplishments would feel, but once you got there, it just didn't prove to bring as much value and good things into your life as you anticipated. This is common, but it can become a problem if you put a lot of hope, effort, and your family's engagement and resources into goals that seem unrealistic to begin with. For example, if you wanted to train ballet, perhaps don't aim to win your first competition within a year. Do some research about the particular goal and find out what amount of time, work, and money is needed to fulfill plans in real-time. If that doesn't work with your desires and abilities, look for the alternatives that are better suited to your current abilities (e.g. modern dance).

Appreciate Your Achievements

Remember to congratulate yourself on meeting weekly, monthly, and yearly goals and expectations. Think about how you want to reward yourself in advance. Depending on the possibilities, talk to your family about a specific reward that you want, like a piece of clothing, a bag, a weekend trip, or a vacation. Rewarding yourself for achieving great things will give you a great deal of motivation and energy moving forward.

Chapter 4:

Look Inside: Why Mindfulness Matters

Teen years can be rough on girls. You juggle a lot between school, friends, hobbies, and family, which can all instill a lot of confusion and stress. Once you become anxious, it's more difficult to enjoy your life, socialize, and learn. Racing thoughts, many of which can get very frightening and confusing, feeling lost and insecure, and feeling detached or like you don't belong are all common signs of distress. However, when you feel chronically stressed out, relaxing isn't easy. You might stay awake late into the night and be unable to fall asleep. Or, you might experience procrastination—the blend of difficulty to concentrate on schoolwork and chores with a simultaneous feeling of drudgery for having to do something you used to love. Followed by unnecessary delays and ultimate stress for being late with assignments and failing at tests, procrastination begins to produce more of the same anxiousness that caused it.

The Wonders of Being Mindful

Whether you're shaken and insecure due to an argument with friends, a challenging situation at home, or you simply feel unhappy with yourself and your life, mindfulness can help!

Mindfulness helps you overcome the most challenging limitations and obstacles, whether they're social, school-related, or more close to home—emotional, economic, and etc. If you're struggling, whether emotionally or with learning, it could be for many reasons. Teenage girls are often fully aware of problems and aches that bug them. The difficult, scary, and painful ideas and memories that burden you cause tension and a bad mood. Mindfulness can help you be kind to yourself, which is especially important if you're an achiever who's hard on herself. If you struggle with school work, or even legal problems and big challenges like illness or pregnancy, mindfulness can help relieve pain and stress associated with these situations and events.

What Is Mindfulness?

Mindfulness is an ability to focus on the present moment and bring awareness to how you feel, what you're doing, and what's happening around you. Still confused? To better understand what mindfulness is, let's define what it's opposed to. Have you ever slept in only to rush through the day with little to no attention to what's happening inside and around you? Think of those days when you're rushing to finish homework for the next class during the current one. Hurry, stress, or overwhelming thoughts about assignments, tests, and to-do's can create a feeling of detachment.

When you're "detached," you stop being aware of your feelings and needs, and you stop noticing others. Instead, you focus on resolving one urgent situation after another. Or, think about how you feel when you're extremely sad for days—you stop paying attention to what goes on in your home and might even forget to eat or take a shower. All of your focus and energy are on one thought or more difficult, negative thoughts. When moods like these persist for several weeks and months, they can make it difficult for you to end this state of mind. You might even want to, but no matter what you do, you find that your thoughts go to a very unhappy place.

When this happens, the best medicine is to, again, become aware of all the things you love and care about, the people who are close to you, and the events that go on around you. If you use mindfulness practices, you can learn exercises that make you feel better when you're standing, moving, sitting, breathing, training, and even writing and drawing.

Mindfulness is a blend of calm, accepting, and gentle techniques to relieve stress when nothing else helps. Mindfulness techniques teach you to live in a present moment, rather than recalling past unpleasant events and dread about failing or being rejected in the future. Mindful exercises can help you replace unproductive mind-wandering and uncontrollable fantasizing with focused, inspired work that will enhance and grow your talents and abilities (Bluth, 2016).

Benefits of Being Mindful

Although the whole purpose of mindfulness is to not anticipate any special outcomes, it's still good to know what you can expect from it.

When you're being mindful, you become less stressed. You're then able to be more productive, whether it's with schoolwork, art, training, or chores. You find it easier to start with activities and stay focused on the work, rather than feeling tired or hungry all the way through. Mindfulness helps you pay attention to how you truly feel and discover what's going on "beneath the surface," which improves your health, well-being, state of mind, and concentration.

Mindfulness techniques, like meditation, yoga, journaling, and art, give you an opportunity to forget about problems for a while and think about life. It helps you nurture curiosity and become kinder and more accepting of yourself. When you're too stressed and you fear that you'll fail at something, you likely start to think and feel really bad about yourself. You might think that you're not smart, pretty, or talented enough to achieve what you wanted. The longer this happens, the bigger chances that your self-esteem will suffer, and you might start to believe in all of these negative things.

How to Practice Mindfulness

Mindful activities are easy to learn and practice. However, you first need a right approach to these activities, and you need to create the right environment for your exercises. First, the place in which you exercise must feel good and calming. You should have enough light, but not too much, and it needs to be warm enough to feel comfortable, but not too much so as to not make you sleepy. Second, you need a comfortable pillow or a chair to sit on, and of course, clothing that is comfortable and neither feels too tight or too loose on your body.

Third, you need the right equipment. If you're practicing yoga or meditation, you might need a mat, while journaling and art will require writing and drawing/painting supplies. Finally, you need time. Don't rush your mindful rituals, but instead devote a chunk of your day just for hanging out with yourself. With that in mind, here are the coolest ideas for mindful activities that you can start doing right now:

Art and Creativity

Have you ever felt like you couldn't put thoughts into words? You're not alone! Luckily, you don't always have to; you can make art! Just take whichever supplies you like—whether it's paint, crayons, or charcoal—and start drawing. You can make this a daily habit or use art to express difficult feelings—it's up to you! Here's how to do it:

Concentrated Art

Concentrated art revolves around painting or drawing specific objects in detail from various angles and using different techniques. What does this do? It shows your brain how to enjoy exploration and immerse itself in curiosity. Concentrated art can help you find beauty in intellectual work and tackling challenges, from paying better attention at school to feeling more comfortable talking to new people.

Spontaneous Art

Spontaneous art is more about not trying to make anything purposeful. It's about not having a goal, restrictions, or directions—just the pure pleasure in expressing whatever you want, however you want it! You can smudge colors on paper or paint whatever comes to mind! Spontaneous art helps you relax and express all of your thoughts and feelings. It doesn't have any boundaries, limitations, or expectations; it's all about what you want to do.

Quiet Contemplation

Quiet 'contemplation,' which simply means 'thinking,' is a process during which you settle down and focus on the inside—your thoughts, feelings, and physical sensations. It's not always easy to find out what really bugs you. People often take their feelings and struggles out on unrelated people and situations. For example, if you're nervous about an argument with your parents and you don't know how to handle all the confusion, anger, and sadness, you might "take it out" on your friends—or the opposite. Some girls don't want to tell their friends that they're upset about something. They either don't want to look weak and vulnerable, or they don't want to cause a fight. Instead, they release their frustration at home, often by snapping at their siblings and being spiteful with their parents. You can see how this is unhelpful. You basically double the conflict instead of resolving the one that exists. Quiet contemplation helps you "connect the dots" and find out what really upsets you, whether it's self-consciousness about your looks or something that someone said. That way, you can "work things out" with yourself and find out what you truly think and feel—before you confront anyone else. Or, if you're too shy to speak out about things that bother you, quiet thinking can help gain security and courage. Here are the exercises to do it:

Meditation

Meditation is done by simply sitting down in a quiet room, closing your eyes, and relaxing as you breathe in and out of your belly—not your lungs, though, because this will make you feel dizzy. Here are the steps:

1. Find a quiet place to sit down and relax. Tune out any noises and distractions from your phone or TV. Make sure that the light is dimmed or that blinds and curtains are closed.
2. Sit down and straighten your back. Place your palms on top of your thighs. Begin breathing.
3. Breathe evenly, with each breath filling up your stomach.
4. As you breathe, try observing the thoughts that come to mind—but don't think about anything specific. Just let your mind wander.
5. Just note what the thought is, and let it pass.

6. Are you afraid that you'll think or see something upsetting? Take a deep breath and let the fear out. It's just the brain—it can't produce anything that will have a real effect on you.
7. Breathe and note your thoughts between five and thirty minutes.
8. Gently open your eyes.
9. Rest for a few minutes, and then try to remember the thoughts that you noted. Try to connect them with situations, people, or memories that made you feel a certain way.
10. If you're in the mood, write down your observations.
11. Don't try to follow how your thinking or behavior changed after meditation—that's not the point. Meditation is a simple way to "drain" negativity; don't spend your entire day thinking about it.

Mindful Walks

Spending too much time in your room and in front of screens can make you nervous. Have a lonely walk each day somewhere safe and in nature for 15 minutes to an hour. Use this time to observe nature, buildings, and people. Think about the landscape, its history, or memories that tie you to the location. Then, when you're ready, start a "walking meditation." It's done in the same way as regular meditation, only with your eyes open. While walking, spend a couple of minutes observing your thoughts and then focus on how your neck, shoulders, back, and legs feel. If you feel tense, focus on the tingling sensation in your calves and feet, and think about how all of the negativity is draining into the soil.

Breathing Exercises

Rushing through life without taking the time to rest and relax can hurt the way you breathe. Correct breathing—and yes, breathing *can* be incorrect—can give you headaches, nightmares, fatigue, and overall make you feel grumpy and sluggish. Many girls don't breathe accurately because they sit at their school desk for a long time or at home when studying and watching TV. When you sit, you slouch. When you slouch, you can't breathe into your belly, as you should. Instead, you start pumping air directly into lungs. This creates pressure in your lungs that doesn't allow them to work properly. This causes all the negative effects mentioned above. But, there is worse. If you're snoring and having nightmares, this is also tied with disrupted breathing. Learning how to breathe into your belly again will improve your mood and reduce anxiety. If you persist with these exercises for several months, your automatic breathing will change into its natural form, and you'll no longer have to work on it. Here's how to do a breathing exercise:

1. Take a three-second breath into your belly.
2. Hold for three seconds.
3. Breathe out slowly, for three more seconds.
4. You should do this exercise for only a couple minutes the first few days. Then, you can add five more minutes each day until you get to 30 minutes. After that, your exercises should last for about 30 minutes.
5. Practice in different positions, altering between sitting, lying on your bed, and standing each day. This trains your brain to command correct breathing in different positions.

Focused Awareness

Remember all of the thoughts and feelings that you noted during walks, meditation, and art sessions? Probably not. Catching the truly tricky thoughts takes work. Those good voices that tell you all about how great you are and how much beauty there is to life and people escape under pressure, while the bad ones take over—the ones that say that you're "always embarrassing yourself," you're "ugly," or you don't deserve to be loved and successful. Concentrated thinking helps you get to the bottom of all that mess, but getting your mind in order takes a bit of writing. Because of this, you should use techniques like the following:

Journaling

Buy a nice-looking notebook and take some time each evening to write down what your day looked like: what you did, who you met, how these experiences made you feel, and what you thought in these situations. Let your mind do its magic and write whatever you want until you feel like no words remain unwritten. Beware of the internet though. Don't write an e-journal, because there's always a possibility that someone gets to your writing and uses it for wrong purposes. Worried about how to keep your journal private? Choose a spot where you know your siblings won't look and that's hard to get to like under the mattress, the bottom of a dresser drawer, or a memento box that you keep in your closet.

Gratitude

Writing down all the things that you appreciate each day will give you that precious dose of joy when times are rough. Write down everything that you're thankful for, with no limitations. It can be your family, health, friends, teachers, nature, your favorite flower—anything that sparks joy and happiness.

Noting Sensations

Sometimes, you'll get upset and won't have the time to "walk it off." In these situations, take a couple of minutes to yourself and write down two columns: one listing what you think and the other listing the specific feelings and sensations that these thoughts create. True, doing this in school, in front of everyone, can make you look strange and draw unwanted attention. If you're not in a very open-minded environment, you can go to the restroom and do your writing there, after which you can tear out the piece of paper and flush it down the toilet.

What Mindfulness Isn't: Traps to Avoid

Sadly, there are some negative sides to practicing mindfulness. If you do it with too many expectations, like to become cooler, smarter, and more confident really quickly, you might lose track of what it's all about: getting to know and love yourself. Even sadder, mindfulness has become such a developed industry that not everyone who profits from it has good intentions. Here are traps to avoid when practicing mindfulness:

The Abuse of Trust: Beware of Predatory Mentors/Scammers

As mentioned, mindfulness became an industry in which company owners make a lot of money. The true, useful knowledge about mindfulness comes from science, but it can be manipulated for malicious purposes.

The first and most obvious risk is buying useless products. Remember, mindfulness is something you do for yourself—it can't be "done" for you by a book, a class, a hypnosis tape, or a membership in a club. Don't buy anything related to mindfulness without permission from your parents. Let them review the product first and decide whether you truly need it. Most of the time, you can get what the product promises for free—by doing it on your own.

The second and potentially biggest risk comes from engaging in malicious communities that present themselves as mindful and supportive but are instead predatory. Nowadays, there are thousands of people presenting themselves as teachers, gurus, and mentors. You can find them in any child-related industries, from sports to extracurriculars. The basic "tell" that a person or an organization is shady is that they insist on separating you from your parents. No self-respecting expert will ask their student to keep secrets from their parents or to meet one-on-one outside regular classes or counseling. Your parents should run a background check on anyone who tutors you, and you should be open and honest about what goes on during training and activities. The same way some predators want to entice girls into drinking or taking substances or try and molest them, fake mentors aim to gain girls' trust to engage in inappropriate activities.

Finally, some teachers who charge for their services are simply false. They don't have any certification to teach mindful practices or they falsify their degrees. Anyone can finish an online class and call themselves a mentor, but not everyone is good at it. Don't pay anything on your own using your allowance or your parent's credit cards. Instead, let them make the decision that's best for you.

Overthinking

You don't have to do all the activities listed above. Select a couple that work best. Mindfulness shouldn't become an obsession, no matter how fun it is. It serves to help you get rid of anxiousness, not to "police" your thoughts and feelings so that you can write them down when the time comes. Overthinking will confuse you even more and might even worsen already existing fears and insecurities.

Escaping Reality

Both children and adults sometimes rely too much on mindfulness exercises. They spend too much time contemplating and too little time actually living the same life that they're trying to improve. Don't let this happen! Mindfulness can get addictive if you use it to escape from challenging thoughts and situations rather than confront them with acceptance and kindness.

Chapter 5:

Achieve and Thrive: How to Get Motivated

Do you want to look and feel great? Do you want to have good grades? Do you want to train, be creative, win a competition, and earn rewards? Do you want to live a happy, fulfilling life? In earlier chapters, you learned about a couple of things needed to get there—having mindful awareness about what you want and what makes you happy and being hard-working and organized. But, that's not all—you're only half-way through the journey.

Here, in Chapters 5 to 11, you'll find out what most teenagers don't know: how to single-handedly give your work a higher meaning and overcome every man and woman's worst enemy—themselves.

Motivation: What It Means and Why It's Important

As mentioned in Chapters 3 and 4, great things are always easier said than done. Let me tell you about how my dream, even in the best of circumstances, quickly turned into a major difficulty that I had to overcome. Now, you know how important it is that your home looks and feels nice to be in. Most girls love to decorate their rooms, as do adult women. Throughout my entire young life, I coped with never fully being able to afford a home that would look just the way I wanted. Fast forward some decade-and-half, and I worked hard enough to save for a house renovation. Imagine my pleasure when I was able to transform my home the way I wanted my entire life. Yet, when the time came to actually do it, it was a ton of work that made that six months of my life pure hell. When I had imagined my perfect home, I hadn't been thinking about having walls and floors stripped or having to coordinate contractors so that I wouldn't live both without a bathroom and a kitchen while they got their work done. I also didn't think about having to clean, tidy, and run my life each day in what could easily be described as a torn-down home. Even in the best of circumstances, making my dream come true was hard and demanding. The result? Mine and my family's endless happiness with a fully renovated house, with each piece in place for comfortable living. The road there? Ouch—so difficult, exhausting, and scary.

What kept me going through having to manage work, kids, and all the construction work? The right kind of motivation!

The Meaning of Motivation

Motivation is an awareness of a very important 'WHY,' the deep purpose that drives everything that you do. There are many things that motivate you, from wanting to earn something material (e.g. shopping or a trip) to wanting to feel successful (e.g. good grades). But, being motivated isn't always easy, and not all of us are driven by the same things. However, without motivation, it's impossible to do anything truly good or productive. Motivation feels like an inner batter that juices you up to do something, no matter how hard it is. The sensation of joy over a satisfying outcome is so intense that it often keeps your attention off of the difficulty of the actual work—whether it's a difficult essay, preparing for a sports competition, or making five paintings of the same orange to win a spot in your desired class.

What Motivation Is (Li et. al., 2021):

- **Knowing your goal.** There are many hard, boring things that you'll have to do to get the one thing you're after. Schoolwork, homework, chores, and extracurriculars often feel mundane and pointless. But, they have a role to play in what you're trying to achieve. Some of these things don't directly link with your goal but instead train your focus and mental resilience. For example, math homework doesn't look very useful if you're pursuing art or sports. However, going through all of those annoying tasks, exercising over and over again, prepares you for the same repetition that you'll need for drawing the same scene multiple times or repeating an exercise until you've done it spot-on. To motivate yourself to do many things that you don't like, first discover what role they have in your general and specific goals. Need help? Turn to your parents and teachers.

- **Knowing how to get there.** If achieving your goal looks impossible or you only have a vague idea about how to do it, it will cause confusion and unnecessary fears. To avoid this, talk to your parents, teachers, and instructors and find out what's realistically needed for what you're trying to achieve.

- **Overcoming frustration.** The reason you're working toward a new goal is that you want to achieve something that you currently don't have, which also means that you still don't know enough about it. A lot of the time, we think that a sheer volume of work will be enough or that our talents will "pull the weight" instead. Learning, getting, and achieving something new will mean learning new skills—and that's hard! Knowing that you'll get frustrated at the challenge and having the willingness to work through this frustration will strengthen your motivation.

What Motivation Isn't:

- **Doing things for wrong reasons.** Have you ever felt that gut-wrenching feeling of "Why isn't this making me happy?" Whether you got invited on a date by your crush or all of your friends turned up for your birthday party, great outcomes feel bad when done for wrong reasons. If you wanted both of the above things not because you wanted to bond with those people (right motivation), but because you wanted attention and to feel worthy (wrong motivation), it will never be enough.

- **Running on 'autopilot.'** Perhaps you do many, if not all, things in life "just because." You never thought about what they mean to you or gave them much thought. Hard work without a purpose in mind is bound to make you unhappy!

- **Fear of failing or missing out.** Doing things just because "everyone else is doing it" is also bound to fail or at least leave you feeling empty and unhappy. It's ok to like the same things that everyone else does, but it's not ok to put energy, work, and allowance into things that don't mean anything to you.

Why Do You Need Motivation

Now, it's time to look deeper and find out what kind of motivation you need to get ahead. If you struggle in certain areas in your life, whether it's school, chores, or social life, decide to work on motivation now to avoid long-term consequences. Remember, all of the things that you need to do as a teen are necessary for lifelong happiness—even if it doesn't appear so. Here's why it's necessary to discover your true driving force:

- **Personal and mental strength.** Remember that bit of personal experience I shared earlier? Even the most amazing things in life will take a lot of work and devotion. Fairytale wedding? You'll need to earn a ton of money first to be able to afford it, then spend months picking and choosing each item and detail, and then organize and plan out the entire event. Being good-looking and healthy will entail taking good care of yourself daily, which will mean doing your hair and make-up, planning outfits, and getting out to train even when you don't feel up for it. Mental discipline and strength are needed to simply decide to do things that you don't want to because they're "the right thing to do" and so that you can relish in the fabulous, rewarding fruit of your labor afterward.
- **Achievement.** Motivation directly decides how well you'll do in life. I know that future plans aren't high on your priority list, but motivation applies to short-term goals as well. If you have a specific GPA in mind, keeping up with all of the tests, assignments, and projects will mean staying in when everyone else is having fun and getting out of bed to study even if you're sad or sick. Motivation is the only thing that will keep you going during hard times.
- **Fulfillment.** Had I wanted to renovate my home just to "keep up with the Joneses," it's very likely that I wouldn't have had

mine and my family's needs in mind but instead just wanted to compete with others. I might have pushed the project too fast and things would have been done poorly or I would have been miserable the entire time. I would never have felt as fulfilled with the result as I have by putting my heart in it. In the same way, fulfillment will only happen to you if you're driven by the goal's deeper meaning.

What Happens When You're Not Motivated

Being unmotivated is even worse than having superficial motivation. The lack of motivation, even if only in one area of your life, will make you feel guilty, sad, and frustrated. Here are the main risks of doing things without motivation:

Drudgery

You may not like school. Yet, you HAVE to go to school; not liking it won't change that. Now, ask yourself, is sitting through lessons feeling bored to death useful to anyone? You can't escape it! You may no longer want to do sports, but what's the alternative? Will sitting in front of the TV really make you feel better? Giving up on things for the lack of motivation will leave an empty place in your heart that will fill up with frustration very quickly.

Failure

No matter how hard you try, achieving your goals will ultimately become impossible without a driving force. Only when you fail and learn about all the things that you've lost will the true benefit of having persisted through hardship reveal itself. Have you ever sat on a bus on your way home, looked at your D-, and just thought, "This could have been a B if I just studied for two more hours!" Yet, rewind back to the night before the test, and not catching up with your favorite TV show seemed like such a loss. Yet, had you resisted the temptation, you could have enjoyed a fair-earned TV time with a grade to be proud of by your side. Now, you are thinking about how to bring the grade back up before the holidays, and life just becomes more stressful, doesn't it?

Unhappiness

Without a purpose or a goal in mind, everything you do will feel like torture. You'll feel constantly unhappy, up until the point of not seeing the point of ever striving or wanting to achieve.

Unfulfilled Achievement

Even if you do achieve a goal without the right motivation, you'll feel like a queen sitting on her throne—all alone. The reward just won't bring the right sort of happiness into your life.

How to Boost Motivation

Finding motivation, and keeping it, isn't difficult; it just takes doing some self-reflection and thinking about your goals. Here are a couple of ways to do that:

Visualize Goals

Imagining how achieving the goal will feel is exciting, but you won't always be able to do it. When you're supposed to study with a headache or go to training on a rainy afternoon that was just made for getting cozy on the couch, you'll need something more—something in-your-face that will remind you of what you're doing in life. Visualization can be done in numerous ways, and here are my top picks:

- **A vision board.** If you've written down all of your general and specific goals, turn them into images. Browse online and find quotes and pictures that closely resemble your future vision, a.k.a what will your goal look like when achieved. Then, get a nice board that you can hang close to your desk or somewhere in your room that you can clearly see no matter what you're doing. Add your chosen images to the vision board, and you'll not only have an amazing piece of decor, but also daily inspiration for everything that you'll be trying to do.

- **Stickers and images.** You can take your motivation with you wherever you go! Again, if you're not in an open-minded environment regarding self-development, you can get decorative quotes and images in the form of stickers, pendants, charms, and even printed school supplies! My favorite trick was to add pins or stickers with positive, uplifting quotes to my folders, and later office files, whenever it was possible and appropriate. That way, you'll stay aware of the 'WHY' in the moment, while you're doing the work and experiencing challenges.

- **Role models.** Finding someone amazing to look up to, reading their biographies, and learning about their life is a major motivator. The best part is you don't have to have just one role model! I looked up to my late grandmother for courage and resilience, my grandfather for his amazing creative and business skills, my father for his leadership traits, and my mother for parenting and personal life. Those were the people I found to be most successful, as their lives were closest for me to learn from. But, you can also look up to leaders from your own environment or community, scientists, philosophers, politicians, TV personalities, and anyone else who inspires you!

Face Problems

Whoever you choose to learn from, you'll find that they had to overcome a storm of obstacles to be who they eventually became. Tesla came from poverty, Einstein had learning difficulties, and Oprah faced abuse, poverty, and psychological adversity. There's no single person alive who doesn't go through adversities, but the successful ones don't let them get in the way. You too should take a look at what your adversities are, think of realistic ways to work around them, and simply decide that those obstacles won't stop you.

Overcome Fear of Failure

Failure will always be both a risk and a reality with achieving the goal of a fulfilled life. You are striving for what you want but currently don't have—and you also need a set of whole new skills. Failure will come in the form of being rejected, being passed at auditions or for teams, or losing at a competition. But, hey, that's life! Usually, the staples that mark success are granted to few of many interested girls, like spots at teams, school plays, and competitions. That simply means that you need to work harder, try again, and make multiple entries to multiple places before your talent is noticed. That's OK! Failure shows you what you need to correct and perfect—nothing more!

Have a "Contingency Plan"

The so-called "contingency plans" are worst-case scenarios with plans for how to prevent and cope with them. Adult experts and business people use them to plan for how to face situations that could jeopardize their plans. With motivation, a "contingency plan" would mean figuring out steps to prevent loss of motivation and planning out steps to pick yourself up when you start to feel down. Here's an example:

Worst Case Scenario: Getting Sick a Before a Competition
1. **Prevention:**
    a. Have a "clean" daily schedule at least 10 days before: no parties, no junk-food, no staying up late, no risky activities that would cause an injury.
    b. Apply to multiple competitions with close-enough dates so that you can enter the next one if the first one fails.
    c. Learn about alternative possibilities to enter late(r) or participate with another group.
2. **Preparation:**

a. Stock up vitamins, medicines, fruits, pre-make green smoothies, and react as soon as you feel the first symptoms.

b. Collect all of the needed paperwork in case you need to change your plans.

c. Check your doctor's office hours so that you can get an appointment as soon as possible.

3. **Intervention:**

a. Quick recovery: Talk to your parents about different options for healing, like medication, supplements, or physical therapy.

b. Damage control: Applying for alternative competitions quickly and without delay.

c. Get back on your feet when you're ready and pick up with preparations.

d. If there are no alternatives, set a couple of days aside to process your feelings and come to terms with loss. Write in your journal, spend time with friends and family, and do whatever you can to feel better.

Chapter 6:

Focus

You only need to study for two more hours, and you're done! But, you're suddenly thirsty. As you come back from the kitchen, you feel like you need to use the bathroom. Right after you're done and back at your desk, your stomach suddenly starts growling. You want to read and revise, but you constantly feel the need to check your phone. You feel hungry, thirsty, tired, bored, and all of those things—while trying to focus. What's happening?

Find Your Purpose: What is Your "WHY?"

There are many reasons why we lose focus. Sometimes, what we're doing is boring. We don't like it. Other times, focusing is just too hard. You might like your reading or find the assignment inspiring, but you just feel drained after writing a couple of notes. Some of the reasons behind the loss of focus are

- **Rush and lack of preparation.** Perhaps, you didn't leave enough time to finish your work, and now you're cramming it at the last minute. Deep down, you know that there's no chance of doing it well, and instead of admitting that, you're trying to do the impossible. Or, you haven't been thinking about your needs, so you didn't get a nice meal and enough rest beforehand. Thus, you can't focus because you are, indeed, tired and hungry.
- **Insecurity.** Perhaps, deep down, you don't feel capable of finishing the task? Or, you are a perfectionist, and you feel tense because you know you won't be able to meet your high standards. All of these feelings can make you feel insecure. You

might struggle to focus because you already feel like you failed and that working any further is pointless.

- **Missing out.** Yes, it's terrible to stay in and rest before a competition while everyone else is going to a party. Knowing what you're missing can keep your mind on other things, and make it hard to concentrate.

But, regardless of circumstances, focus is necessary for success, achievement, and happiness. The best and only way to focus when you can't seem to do something is to cope with unpleasantness and make a conscious decision to follow through without commitment. That decision is based on having a clear purpose in mind and thinking about that purpose whenever a distraction happens.

Discover Your Purpose

The word 'purpose' can mean many things when applied to focusing and motivation. In this sense, it is more than a reason for doing something. It's also a cause, a feeling of something "being right." When tasked with doing or reading something and having problems with concentration, knowing the purpose of your work can quickly bring you back on track. To discover the inner sense of purpose for your work, ask yourself the following questions:

- What does this do for me?
- How does my work benefit others?
- How does my work benefit mankind?
- How does the task serve my values and goals?
- What will happen if I complete my work?
- What will happen if I give up?

As you can see, the purpose that comes out of your answers won't be a single word. It will be a whole insight into the importance of what you're doing as well as the consequences of giving up.

Live By Your Values

Think about everything you value in life and write it down. Most frequent values among people are honesty, goodness, love, family, community, etc. But, people often don't put effort into living by their values. What does this have to do with focus? A lot of the time, engaging in inspired work evokes a feeling of guilt. How do you get to sit comfortably in your room and read when you haven't helped around the house? Or, you might start to think about the underprivileged and feel like you shouldn't enjoy work because you haven't earned it by being good. Guilt only worsens if you procrastinate and give up—so don't let that happen! Instead, write down your most important values and then decide on one to three things that you can realistically do each day that manifest that value. You'll never be truly able to live up to your ideals, but you will earn your own respect, and this will alleviate a lot of stress when you're doing expired work.

Find Out What Moves You

Take some time to reflect on "what makes you want to do things." Similar to inspiration, this can vary from girl to girl. Think about the time when you did a lot of work without stopping. What was on your mind? What were you looking forward to? For some girls, it's a reward of some sort or a satisfying outcome. For others, it can be working with colorful supplies or knowing that they'll soon take a break and have a snack. Once you know what makes the work feel worth the trouble, you'll have an easier time focusing.

Declutter the Mind and Gain Clarity

Aside from feeling nervous and insecure, there are many other thoughts and distractions that are making it difficult to focus. Mainly, it's thoughts. Sometimes, you can't focus because all of your energy goes into thinking about other things. Clarity is one of the ways to overcome this. Having a clear mind means feeling calm, for starters. It also means to learn to let go of distractions and stressful thoughts. But, this too is hard. We can't really take out thoughts from our hands and throw them into trash. That's not how brains work. Instead, we need to learn how to quiet them and simply ignore—at least temporarily—those thoughts that aren't helpful.

Clarity isn't about clearing your mind of thoughts but choosing to put forward only those thoughts that you need at the moment and "turn away" from all else. But, this isn't easy. Distracting thoughts are most often about things that we want to do but can't, things we want but can't have, things that we're afraid of, and things that we don't want to happen. When these thoughts pair up with real-world distractions, like TV, music, or pings from your phone, they become impossible to manage! To become able to concentrate on your work and activities and not get distracted easily, you need to first declutter your mind and then find the right things to focus on.

Why Are Your Thoughts Racing?

Difficulties with concentration most often happen when you think about too many things at once—it's that simple! Have you ever poured liquid through a funnel? Think about the narrow tube as your ability to concentrate and the wide part as the rest of your mind. If you ever baked a cake or participated in a science project, you know that pouring too much liquid into the funnel causes it to block. On top, you have a dish full of the substance, but there's nothing coming out on the other side. The same goes for your brain—dealing with too many issues causes mental blockage.

When your mind is overwhelmed with too many issues, it will have trouble operating, just like any other mechanism. One of the simpler solutions to concentration is to avoid overwhelm. In the above example, you need to add liquid slowly so that it can drain on the other side. In your mind, you need to work through issues that bother you and relieve stress before getting to work. The process for this is simple, and it's all about doing everything you can to calm down and relax, among other things.

How to Declutter the Mind

As I mentioned earlier, decluttering the mind is a lot like making a choice between thoughts and ideas that you want to keep and those that you want to let go of. For example, while reading, you might find yourself thinking about something that your frenemy said in class, other assignments that you need to do, or about failing tomorrow's test. While these thoughts represent real insecurities that you should deal with, the current moment—when you're supposed to be learning—is not the right time. So, what do you do next?

You need to remind yourself that these negative thoughts are completely useless. My favorite trick is to say to myself, "I'll get to that later" or just "Later." The emphasis here is on "later," which is much more effective than trying to avoid or suppress your scary thoughts. By acknowledging that you will tend to them later when the time is right, you are sending your brain a message that you'll get to the bottom of these issues and there's no need for it to insist on them so hard. But, you also have to own up to that promise. Make it a habit to write a journal in the morning and evening and address negative thoughts, feelings, and insecurities. Be really honest with yourself and don't hold back. You may not be able to resolve all problems, but you will acknowledge them and remove the need for your brain to constantly send these distracting mental pings. Think of this process as opening a message without reading. Doing this removes the notification from your screen and shuts down the distracting lights and pings that serve as a reminder. However, if you don't want to miss out on important information, you also need to find the time to read and respond to the messages that you received.

Gain Clarity: Focused Relaxation

Now that you know how to regain focus quickly when needed, it's time to learn to clear your mind long-term. Many things that you learned in earlier chapters will help with this, like journaling, organization, and mindfulness. Doing all of these things will help you learn what bothers you, what causes anxiousness, and how to let go. However, learning to use focused relaxation to willingly give up on negative thoughts will help you eventually overcome problems with concentration and strengthen your willpower.

Focused relaxation means to focus on one calming thing and relax while observing it. This helps you truly forget about negativity while learning to concentrate. Indeed, not all things that you'll need to focus on will be pleasant, but you will train your mind to do what you want it to do. Focused relaxation is different from meditation, although there are some similarities. First, you need to get yourself in a quiet, pleasant space with soft lighting. Then, you need to pay attention to an object in front of you. This object should invoke calm and happiness. Some people like to look at plants or flowers, while others choose a tree, fountain, or a hill in the distance. Personally, I like to light a candle and look at the flame. Then, as you observe the object, you should do a breathing exercise as described earlier in the book. You can practice focused relaxation for as long as you like.

Sometimes, you will feel some negative thoughts coming back right after you finish the exercise or sometime later. You should address them from a calm state of mind, one by one, either by thinking or journaling. You might notice that, over time, you become able to simply say, "I don't care about this anymore." The more you practice focused relaxation, the easier it becomes to do that whenever necessary.

Last Minute Call: Overcome Procrastination!

It's evening time, and you're supposed to start doing your homework. If you start on time, you can finish in less than two hours and then enjoy some reading or TV. But, you find it difficult to start. You lie on your bed, looking at your desk, thinking about reasons why you don't have to start yet. You suddenly want to have a snack and take a shower. Before long, you start to feel like there's no need to do anything at all—you can simply get up earlier or catch up with homework on the bus. The result? You sadly discover that your homework is much more difficult than it looked. No matter how badly you wish to have done it on time, there's no way to fix the damage—you're now facing a lower grade than you could have gotten if you hadn't procrastinated. Lack of concentration isn't the only problem that you'll face. Procrastination, or a habit to delay work, bugs both teenagers and adults. It is a common problem and the most frequent cause of failure at work and in school.

Why Do We Procrastinate?

The same reasons behind problems with concentration cause procrastination. Sometimes, you're overwhelmed, and you know in advance that your plans aren't irrealistic. Other times, you fear that you're missing out, and you don't start studying or working on your project on time. At its core, procrastination is fear that the task will be too much for you.

Why Is Procrastination Bad?

Over time, procrastination leads to many negative outcomes. Some are obvious, like low school grades and the opportunity for them to reflect your full potential. Other side-effects of procrastination leave a permanent mark on your health and well-being. Procrastinating puts you in a vicious cycle of failure—you delay and then get disappointed by the lack of achievement, which increases your insecurity and creates even more procrastination, failure, and so on. Anyone who works with children and teens knows that each boy or girl is a magical source of endless potential. But, that potential can show itself and manifest in success, achievement, and personal happiness only through work. Despite having an essay all figured out in your head, you still have to write it, right? You might have, in your mind, composed a most beautiful melody, but you still need to master playing the instrument if you want others to enjoy it as well. Procrastination steals that opportunity from you because it weakens your physical and mental potential.

How to Overcome Procrastination

As someone who suffered from procrastination herself, I can confirm that the ultimate way to truly overcome it is "cold-turkey"—just stop doing it. The anguish that you'll experience at the beginning of your work is bound to go away within 10–30 minutes, and then you'll start enjoying even the most demanding tasks. Have you ever taken a test, looked at the question, and felt like you didn't know a single answer? That's nervousness blocking your mind, but the clock is ticking, and you just start writing answers because you have to. Then, after one or two questions, you finally calm down and start remembering everything you've learned. The same will happen after you just hop right into doing your task or chore. The first few minutes will be excruciating. You might start to sweat, your throat might feel dry, and you might even start to tremble. As someone who's had that happen to them at the beginning of a really long house cleaning session, I guarantee that the anguish will go away!

However, beating procrastination isn't a "one-time thing." Procrastination is a habit, and as such, you have to alter a series of habits to strengthen your willpower, because it will sneak up on you every time you're not in your best shape.

To banish procrastination from your life forever, think about what leads up to it. Perhaps you lay back for an hour after dinner, and that makes you too tired to study later? Or, you stay up late, and then you're tired and drowsy the entire next day? Many students cram their studies the night before, thinking that there's no use to studying earlier because "they'll forget it anyway." In this case, you need to keep up with your studying schedule and go over the schoolwork at least once each day—which shouldn't take too long.

Preparation is key to avoid procrastination, so think about what you need to not feel like you have to delay your work. Eat on time, tidy your room in the morning, and have a shower right after you get home. If you crave some entertainment, watch an episode of a TV show that you like before the designated learning time. That way, your basic needs are met, and there are no obstacles to doing what you need to. Finally, let me share a hack that worked wonders for me when I lacked time: Do a little bit of work earlier. For example, if you need to study for a test, read through your notes briefly on the schoolbus or in the car. Then, take a quick skim before dinner. Or, if you hate cleaning your room, dust off your desk and a couple of shelves in the morning—when you still don't HAVE to. That way, you'll familiarize yourself with the work beforehand, and it won't look so big and scary when the time comes to actually do it.

Chapter 7:

Empowerment: Find Your Strength

Do you want to feel powerful and like you're capable of doing things that are important to you without obstacles? Yet, something is holding you back. You struggle to stand up for yourself, and you figure out funny comebacks long after an argument is over—does this sound familiar? The feeling of personal power makes a person feel strong, capable, and in control. But, in its absence, both teens and adults feel afraid, confused, and insecure. Feeling powerless is one of the root causes of anxieties, insecurities, depression, and many other mood disorders. Even if it doesn't affect you significantly, it might create this feeling like the world is a big monster that's forever after you, hostile, unpredictable, and unsafe. Because of this feeling, you might have overwhelmingly negative thoughts that ruin your happy days, friendships, and love life.

What Personal Power Is and How to Embrace it

Personal power can mean two different things. Some people think that having personal power means having the ability to influence others—how they feel and what they do—to your advantage. However, people like myself, who have come to learn that that's not how one gains happiness, have a different take on personal power—one that draws from psychology and relates to people's mental health.

Looking at it from the fulfillment and happiness perspective, personal power is a core feeling that you're capable and competent of protecting yourself, looking after yourself, and doing important things. As such, it includes independence, strength, knowledge, and skills. Girls who feel powerful believe in their own abilities, but that belief doesn't come out of nowhere. Feeling powerful comes from learning, practicing, gaining experiences, and making things happen.

Personal Power: The Key to Health and Happiness

Why is personal power crucial for health and happiness? If you feel powerLESS, then you feel like your life fully depends on others. You rely too much on other people's help, approval, and acceptance. However, getting help and acceptance from others never truly relieves powerlessness. You may not be aware that you feel that way, but you might fear that your friends will all abandon you, like you don't know what to do when your parents or siblings aren't around, or like you can't manage an assignment on your own unless a classmate or a teacher is providing assistance. At first, core powerlessness might feel similar to being insecure, but it's much more intense and scary. Girls who feel powerless are often afraid without a real cause. For example, they fear that someone will break into their home each night, that their friends will turn on them, or that their boyfriends will leave them. This state of mind is constant, and it's always fear of one bad outcome or another. Powerlessness is different from anxiety, even though they both manifest in fears. However, with anxiety, people fear ridicule, failure, or embarrassment, and the fear is more related to shame. With powerlessness, the fear concerns an actual idea that someone or something will hurt you, and it's there no matter what you do.

Some girls with these issues cope using aggression. They snap at the smallest provocation because they fear being endangered. Others are too shy and withdrawn and let others "walk all over them." There are also girls who we often call "fake." They put on a "persona" that they feel is desirable but keep their thoughts and intentions to themselves, often hurting others in an effort to gain power. Such girls are those who scheme, plot, and gossip behind others' backs.

As you can see, neither of the scenarios makes it easier on the girl to have healthy, loving friendships and relationships. People who have a feeling of true personal power feel undoubtedly capable of keeping themselves safe and protected, no matter the age. They understand that there are real dangers out there, but they don't assume the worst in people. They are rational and cautious, but courageous and driven.

More importantly, they trust other people and don't shy away from healthy bonding. By "healthy bonding," I mean the type of bonding that has reasonable boundaries. They acknowledge people's right to disagree, be hurt, and need space, but they also honor themselves and their dignity. Feeling empowered means believing in your strength and not being afraid that other people will hurt you.

Types of Power and How to Gain It

Personal power comes from skills and capabilities. As such, it can be physical, intellectual, artistic, economic, and in all other forms in which capabilities manifest themselves. Typically, people are neither fully powerless or ultimately powerful. Everyone has strengths and weaknesses. Sometimes, people with enormous intellectual power don't have natural talents or interests in gaining physical power through training and martial arts. So, they obtain influence and economic power and secure themselves the sort of protection that they want by getting a home in a safe, gated community or hiring security guards. Or, people who don't particularly like to read and learn invest their energy into personal power that they use to keep themselves safe, and they eventually profit from doing jobs where physical power is needed. While this does happen often in life, I don't think it's the best way to live. When you don't make an effort to strengthen your skills and knowledge in those areas where you lack, it creates a type of insecurity that will follow you wherever you go. Because of this, some rich people are always paranoid and think that people are after their life or money, and many people with physical power feel insecure in their intellectual skills.

Instead, you can find a balance and challenge yourself to gain strength on all levels—physical, mental, and emotional. While it's great to build power through those activities that match your talents, strengthening those that lack will give you a true feeling of might. You could be eloquent, well-versed, and trustworthy, but what if you added martial arts or construction work to that list, for example? Those areas where you feel the weakest, whether it's sports or talking to others, when strengthened, give a person a true feeling of potency. This feeling fuels your self-esteem, creativity, drive, and motivation. Think of it as the seed from which all of these grow. To plant it, you first need to make a list of "things that you're not good at," and make reasonable efforts to give them a shot.

How to Empower Yourself

While personal power comes from nurturing a sense of personal abilities in the form of skills and talents, empowerment takes a little bit more. Feeling empowered also includes devoting oneself to certain values and causes, being independent and sharp-minded, and working actively on what you feel to be important for the betterment of the world. To compare, with personal power, you uplift yourself by learning new skills and talents. To achieve empowerment, you need to pair that with building and maintaining personal identity and integrity through active work on fulfilling your values. Technically, you work both on improving yourself and society, which then reflects in your charisma, intellect, appearance, style, and many other areas. It is a higher form of personal power in which you determine what to do in order to empower everyone else.

When you hear about empowerment, you most often hear about empowering girls in a certain direction—to fight back when there's bullying, report violence, enter higher-paying professions, become entrepreneurs, and much more. However, empowerment isn't related to a particular cause. You can empower yourself in any desired direction in which you feel that other people in your community need support. You can focus on social injustices, the underprivileged, overcoming discrimination, or ecological causes. You choose! Even better, you get to pave your own, personal way in which you'll work toward what you feel is important. Sadly, a lot of the time (see last section of Chapter 4) the idea of empowerment is used superficially by individuals and groups to gain their own influence and personal power by "talking big" but achieving very little in real life. For example, brands post supportive messages toward certain marginalized groups but do the exact opposite in real life by breaking laws, committing tax fraud (avoiding to pay taxes), or exploiting workers in third-world countries. When strong messages are shared with little knowledge about true empowerment, they can hurt those who they are trying to help. To avoid this in your personal life and social engagement, use the following steps:

Have an (Educated) Opinion

Every adult, whether parent or teacher, wants to see a child who has an opinion. However, when people (particularly children) make strong statements without enough knowledge and with a wrong attitude, they're quickly dismissed. I'll admit, nowadays, it's hard to be certain in your opinion when each day reveals new information. To avoid making strong arguments while being wrong, read and learn thoroughly from reputable sources about topics and causes you're interested in. The simplest example of how empowerment can go wrong are the so-called "Pyramid schemes," or companies that make money simply by having people join their organizations and recruit for them. Although you, as a teen, are unlikely to be their target, you may inadvertently engage with them via social media and insert yourself in unnecessary drama. Why? Because people online are so quick to research and call out suspicious behavior, while being not-too-considerate of everyone's age, you might encounter online bullying simply for engaging with wrong organizations. Fact-check everything and everyone before choosing to associate with them, and do thorough reading on any matter that you choose to speak about.

Be Critical

Don't put "blind faith" into any person or organization. Understand that no one is perfect, and be willing to acknowledge that those who you admire may have imperfections or have made mistakes in the past. This is important because power and empowerment are too often associated with perfection. You might idolize influencers or musicians only to discover that some of the things they said and did go completely against who you believed them to be. If these people were your inspiration from which you drew your own sense of power, learning about their scandals or negative traits can shake your beliefs and make you feel insecure. That's why it's important to take everything said online and in general media with a grain of salt. Don't think that anyone is perfect, neither in looks nor in career and life. However, just because people's "shady backgrounds" or past controversies come to light, it doesn't mean that you have to dismiss them and their work overall. People live in the present, and if someone who you supported did good things in real life, there's still a lot to learn from them.

Why is this important? Earlier generations of teenage girls didn't have social media. We had to wait to catch our favorite singer's song on the radio or drive to the nearest store that had their CD or poster. We idolized these people and thought that they were pure perfection. When online media and social platforms emerged, those same Hollywood stars began to show themselves in a different light. We learned that they too had flaws. That, in itself, isn't bad. What was bad was thinking we could never live up to that propagated ideal of beauty, talent, skill, success, and romance. Similar things happen today with social media influencers often posting photoshopped images and staged videos of their beautifully decorated homes, fairytale weddings, and spotless performances. These posts make young girls feel like their lives are too boring, like they look nothing compared to their idols, and that they're not as smart as them. This isn't true, because influencers follow a carefully designed plan for how to present themselves to spark interest and get attention. While that doesn't erase their talent, it doesn't mean that you should think less of yourself for being "unable to measure up."

Stand Up for Yourself and Others

Teachers, counselors, and other experts who work with teens all agree that standing up for yourself works. Because bullies and anyone else who wants to hurt you do that in order to gain power from themselves, standing up reveals their weaknesses. It reveals that they're not as brave as they want you to believe. Stand up when someone else is being mistreated as well. This empowers you and improves your self-image. It helps the victim as well, because it shows them that someone has their back and that they're not alone. In fact, people who get victimized often report that the worst part wasn't the incident itself, but instead having people stand around doing nothing to help them. By standing up, you demonstrate and affirm justice to yourself and those around you.

Set and Accept Boundaries

Setting and accepting boundaries is all about being clear about what you will and won't allow and accepting others' boundaries without asking "Why?" Some boundaries are beyond question, like the following:

- Personal choices and orientations: People's likes and dislikes, preferences, beliefs, and personal decisions (e.g. who they want to invite out, date, be friends with, etc.) should be honored. However, that doesn't mean that you shouldn't have an opinion regarding these choices and decide about the relationship based on them.
- Physical boundaries: Respect people's private and personal space, as well as their wishes for how they want to be treated, touched, etc. You are also entitled to having boundaries like these and shouldn't have to explain them either. Disrespecting these boundaries or having other people question your boundaries should make you think about whether or not you want to be friends with them.
- Items and belongings: It's simply good manners to avoid going through other people's personal belongings, paperwork, phone, laptop, etc. without their permission. However, these boundaries tend to get blurred in close relationships. Remember, no matter how close you are with someone, you decide what they are and aren't allowed to do with your personal property, and the same goes for your obligation to avoid going through other people's things.

There are also boundaries that vary from person to person. Everyone has different ideas about these things, and your and everyone else's ability to respect them sometimes depends on circumstances. These boundaries include

- What you and others wish to talk about.

- What you do and don't want to do.
- To what degree you and others are willing to explain your words and actions.

What does this have to do with empowerment? Knowing, understanding, and respecting boundaries as much as you can protects your and other people's privacy, as well as personal and mental space. It creates trust between you and others. Many teen girls feel like they have to tell their friends everything, which can get awkward. Have you ever told one friend something sensitive simply because they were there, and then the rest of your group got angry that you didn't tell everyone else? Or, you got upset because some of your friends told each other some things that they didn't wish to tell everyone else, so you felt left out?

Imagine having an 'accident' in the school restroom and having to go to change. If your teacher wasn't respectful of your boundaries, they'd ask you what happened and you might feel uncomfortable talking about it. However, in most cases, it's enough to say that you need to change, and when the teacher respects your privacy, it strengthens trust and the bond between you. Showing respect for people's choices and boundaries, and also not letting anyone cross yours, shows inner strength and integrity. More importantly, respecting boundaries strengthens your self-respect. It makes you feel good in your eyes and think well of yourself.

Chapter 8:

Feel Good: Be Positive and

Resilient

Wouldn't it be amazing if you could feel good every single day? If only that were possible! In reality, you'll have some good, bad, and really ugly days. But, think. What makes a day good or bad? Is it what goes on on the outside, in school and with other people, or your mood—how you feel about these events? You can feel bad on the inside despite positive things happening on the outside. If you feel moody when things are going well, that means that you should pay attention to what's going on with you emotionally. There are, of course, many circumstances that cause chronic negative feelings, like sadness and melancholy, that are out of your control. Losing someone you love, seeing your family go through struggles, or witnessing distressing events in your community can all cause sadness, tension, and fear. Still, learning how to be relationally optimistic, which we'll do in this chapter, will help you go through hard times and start thinking in a more positive direction.

What Affects Your Emotions

If you look at your life from the outside and you feel like things are mainly fine—there are no major problems keeping you from feeling good—but you still struggle to stay positive, there is a chance that certain lifestyle choices affect your mood. If you, like many teenagers, are going through a hard time, the negative influences on your health will only make you feel worse. No matter the circumstances in your life, choosing to do what benefits your health and getting better emotionally is always a good idea. Here's what can affect your mood no matter what's happening around you:

Lifestyle: Diet, Sleep, and Activities

Diet directly affects how you feel. It's not a simple connection, like eating an orange will make you feel happy, or eating an apple will make you fall in love. Sadly, eating spinach won't help grow muscles, at least not right away. The chemical composition of your food affects your gut, and from there, it influences your brain and changes the hormones that get produced and released into your blood. The rules are simple. If you eat junk food, the excess salt and chemicals from it hurt your gut and cause high blood sugar, and as a result, your brain releases stress hormones. Your brain simply detects that there's something bad going on in your body and responds similarly. But, when you eat healthy food, like lean meat and lots of fruit and vegetables, they break down into vitamins, minerals, and fiber. These substances then do good things for your body, like helping build muscles and tissues. They also boost your immune system and serve to create helpful brain chemicals that make you happy, like serotonin and melatonin.

Thoughts and Interactions

Between 80–90% of things we think are the same every day (Verma, 2019). This means that most people, children or adults, simply tell the same story over and over again in their minds. That makes you want to re-think the story that you say to yourself, doesn't it? If your "inner story" is too negative, it will affect your mood. Similarly, how you talk to others affects your mood. This doesn't mean that you have to push fake positivity. You can simply choose to talk less to people that you don't like, whenever you don't have to, and talk more to people that make you feel good. But, the way you talk to people affects your mood as well. A simple "How are you doing?" can go in a million directions. You can say, "Good, I'm taking a break from studying," or "Terrible, I just studied for two hours and got nothing." Think again if you're pushing conversations in a negative or positive direction, and try to lighten up a conversation whenever possible. This will make you feel better as well!

Environment

Your environment affects how you feel, whether by people and events, or merely with its "vibe." There's not a lot that you can do to change your environment. You only control how you react, what you say and do, and, to a large degree, how you think and feel about the outside events. With that in mind, there are simple things that you can do to improve your personal experience within your environment. You can choose what situations and activities to participate in and when to let go and focus on something else. For example, if the entire class seems to be in a bad mood, you don't have to participate in that toxicity. Instead, you can sit at your desk and do some reading.

Music and Media

What you choose to watch and listen to also affects your mood and mindset. Pay attention to whether you're spending too much time on social media, taking in lots of overwhelming information that you don't know what to do about. The link between media and feelings is direct: Consume positive content and you'll feel better, while the opposite will make you feel worse. Understand that informing yourself only about negative events won't help victims at all. Informing and being consumed by a story are different things. Make your playlist more positive and upbeat, and try watching more feel-good movies than you do thrillers and horrors. This will put you in a better mood, in which you'll react to negative news with more compassion instead of fear and rage.

How to Limit Negative Thoughts and Experience More Positive Thoughts

Most people think that being more positive is a matter of choice. All you need to do is "cheer up" and you'll feel better. That's not the case at all. True positivity, the kind of realistic optimism that "works" in all situations, comes from knowing how to process negative thoughts. For example, let's say you're getting ready for school in the morning. You're happy with how you look while still in the house, but as soon as you leave, your confidence starts to drop. You start looking at other girls and comparing yourself with them, and, even worse, you check Instagram and look at all those girls who look amazing thanks to makeup you can't afford and clothes that are above your means. You might experience something similar when you feel confident in your knowledge before a test, but you start to suspect that you'll fail the test nonetheless. That's called insecurity, and everyone has it. So, what's the remedy in situations like these? Playing an upbeat song is unlikely to help, as is writing out encouraging messages or trying to paint your experience into bright colors.

The key to overcoming negativity lies in resilience. Resilience, the strength to accept the negative and still see more positives about the situation, includes the following simple steps (Monroe, 2017):

Rationalize

Is it possible that the perfect Instagram girl had her photos photoshopped, and that she doesn't use thousands of dollars worth of makeup at all? Are other girls TRULY that better than you—in terms of grades, how many friends they have, or how happy they are in their relationships? A lot of the time, we exaggerate negativity. Only when you start to question it using "real world" criteria, you start to notice that things aren't as bad as they seem to be.

Enjoy the Present

Negative thoughts are often about negative future outcomes, while positive ones are about the present. For example, if you think, "I'm not that smart, I'll never have good grades and go to a good college," you are making future predictions. But, do you REALLY know what will happen in the future? You don't know—nobody does. If you act based on negativity, you are living a story in which you've already written a sad ending for yourself. So, try the opposite. Find something to enjoy in each moment, it can be little things. Let's say the rest of the class feels a bit toxic today, so why not pay attention to how nice the classroom looks and how comfortable it is? Or, look out the window and enjoy the scenery. Positivity begins with little efforts to see beauty, fun, and good around you.

Bond

Negativity of all sorts makes girls isolate. But, without people around, real events to participate in, and the emotional connection that comes with sharing "the good and bad," all you're left with are the negative thoughts. From my experience, choosing to be with a friend over hanging out alone has its advantages, as does reaching out to parents when you feel bad. Most girls prefer to be on their own when they're sad, but that only makes things worse. Instead, find someone to talk to, and you'll find that other people know a great deal of information to help you think more positively.

Spend Time Outside

Few things cheer people up like spending time outside, whether it's strolling through the city or walking in nature. Sunshine, air, and people who go about their day all give you many positive topics to think about. I usually find a lot of encouragement when I look at women who pass by me, noticing so many women who are doing well amid the most challenging circumstances. I notice how nice they look and try to guess what they do and what their life looks like. It's a game of course, but for the most part, I'm dissuaded from fearing for the future by seeing so many people who are doing just fine.

How to Channel and Let Go of Negative Feelings

You should never ignore feelings. Don't task yourself with staying positive at all costs, as this only leads to "toxic positivity," the kind of negativity that comes from faking to be alright. The happiest people out there practice self-compassion and acceptance. They know what to do with negative feelings instead of trying to remove or erase them. After a little bit of exercise, you too will know how to face and overcome negativity by accepting it, being kind to yourself, and knowing how to play with it until you shape it into something new and beautiful.

Confide in Loved Ones

People who love you want you to feel good. Your parents or caregivers, teachers, friends, and more people than you could have imagined all want girls like you to be and feel well. One big blessing that comes with being a teenager is that a vast majority of people feel like it's their duty and want to help you. You have more allies than you know, the first ones being your closest friends and family and your teachers. Us girls, whenever challenges arise, want to hide from the world and disappear. But, that's a mistake. Open up to those you trust. They'll advise, protect, and go out of their way to help you feel better.

Art

Even sadness can be beautiful. It can be a dark blue butterfly, with neon pink, purple, and green patches all over it. Or, it can be a rainbow unicorn amid a misty, dark forest. I loved painting my anger as a mighty volcano that sheds lava down the mountain sides. Art can help you shape all negative feelings into gorgeous sculptures. This not only helps you let go of negativity but also helps you learn to see its other side—the one that shows that, no matter what happens, you can always tap into your utmost strengths and overcome challenges.

Music

The right song at the right time, happy or sad, helps you work through difficult thoughts. It already contains melodies and words that describe just how you feel. Music has a special ability to invoke positive feelings amid difficult ones, and that makes it very helpful.

Sports

Physical activity helps keep your mind from difficulties while doing something healthy and beneficial. Playing sports and being active helps release brain chemicals like dopamine and endorphins that relax you and help control and manage fears.

Chapter 9:

Where Happiness Lies: Hobbies and Interests

More Than Quality Time: Why Hobbies and Interests Are Important

Having fun is a big part of growing up, and pursuing hobbies and interests is a great way to do it while growing your personal strengths. Unlike school, hobbies concern what you like to do, whether it's swimming, music, art, writing, or reading. Still, they have great benefits for your growth and development, and even your future! Here's why it's important to turn off screens, get out, and do something fun and creative.

Nurturing Talents and Skills

School has one way of growing your intelligence and talents—through learning about different subjects and doing assignments. But, hobbies and interests are similar in a slightly different way. What you choose to train and do after school revolves around what you like. Some girls train in sports, others sing, dance, do martial arts, or ice-skate. The beauty in hobbies is that they train the same discipline and resilience that schools do, but in a much more fun way. You may think that getting a hobby will keep your attention away from school, but that's not true. Hobbies help you become smarter and more competent in ways that are suited to you as a unique person, while school does so in ways that are known to "work" for most children. Learning new skills takes work, but when you do something that you truly enjoy, exercise is a lot more pleasant.

Spending Quality Time With Friends

On top of what I mentioned previously, learning hobbies and nurturing natural talents and interests brings you closer to other boys and girls who are like you. Most of us felt out of place or like we "didn't belong" while we were growing up. What if you could meet a couple of extra friends who like the same things that you like? Wouldn't that be great? Feeling like you belong and, even better, working together with others with the same interests empowers you and benefits your self-esteem. This will help you feel better, more supported, and more confident.

Building Social Skills

Hanging out with others and working alongside people who you like and trust helps exercise social skills in a more relaxed setting. With each new group, you'll get to know new people, learn how to make small talk, and inquire about other people in likable, light-hearted ways that don't come across as awkward or intrusive. As someone who tried to acquaint themselves with new people and ended up sounding like a detective, I know how hard it is to learn to walk the fine line between fun and too much. It's a taught skill, and after school classes and projects are a great way to gain it!

Find Out What You're Good At

You'll have the best time and most success at your hobbies if you practice what you're actually good at. Don't fall into the trap of doing what's popular or signing up for hobbies just because the rest of your friends are with them. Instead, nurture your individuality and start pursuing your unique interests. The rest of your class all might like playing basketball, but what if you want to learn how to play the piano? One of the goals for this book is to show you that you don't have to settle for what everyone else is doing to be happy. You'll be just fine if you tap into your uniqueness and find out what works best for you! Here's how to find out what your ideal hobby should be:

What Are Your Talents and Strengths?

"What you're good at" depends on many things. People have natural talents and types of smarts that work with some skills better than others. For example, you can have audio, visual, interpersonal, and motor skills developed to different degrees. Most teens have naturally developed some of these areas more than others and have formed talents that manifest in different skills or better grades in certain school subjects. However, you might not be aware of all of your talents. By now, you have a pretty good idea about your strengths, but you need a bigger picture. To find out more about your personal strengths and talents, you can take different tests called "talent tests" or "career aptitude" tests. These tests explore different sides of you and reveal where your talents are. You can talk to your parents and school counselors to find out how to access testing. The results of your tests will show what crafts, hobbies, and sports are the best for you. Then, you can talk to your parents and caregivers about available organizations, courses, or teams that you should join to pursue those interests that best fit your abilities.

What Are Your Skills?

Talent is the potential to be good at something, while a skill is an already formed set of mental and physical operations that enable you to do certain things. For example, drawing well indicates that you might be talented at art. Similar to that, hitting notes while you sing indicates that you might be a talented musician. Your skills show what you're already good at. Skills are numerous and are an asset that you have already developed. Choosing hobbies based on skills that you already have increases your chance of being successful and more satisfied. Sometimes, finding the right hobby means giving up on certain ideas.

You might like what being a dancer would look like, but if your fine motor skills aren't at the level needed for it, you'll have to work twice as hard to learn dancing. List the skills that you already have and give them a realistic view. Decide what hobby to choose based on what you already know how to do, and enjoy!

What Do You Like to Do?

In an ideal world, what you're talented for, what you already know how to do, and what you like to do would be the same things. But, a lot of the time it's not. Sometimes, we like how certain hobbies and crafts look more than we actually enjoy doing them. For example, when I was a teen, I was fascinated with woodwork. I'd sneak into my grandfather's woodshop and watch him make gorgeous closets and kitchens. However, the more I looked, the more I realized that I wouldn't like all of the noise and debris that come with the territory. I realized that I liked my hobbies to be a bit cleaner, safer, and more relaxing—not that you shouldn't pursue woodwork if you like it, of course. But, being honest with yourself about what you truly like and dislike will help you discover what activities will feel good even when they become challenging. Write a list of things that you like to do, and then compare it with what you found to be your skills and talents.

Finally, your list of suitable activities and hobbies should be a well-measured combination of what you like, what you can do, and what you're good at. After that, you should look at what available activities and courses best fit your inclinations.

Fun for the Future: How to Use Interests to Advance in Life

Hobbies have a potential to turn into a life-fulfilling career. Right now, you're in a great position to build yourself up in a desired direction. You have few obligations and commitments, and you can use all of your time working on yourself to ensure a happy future. Working on your hobbies and interests can grow into a college scholarship or funding to participate in education programs that benefit your future career and employment. Extracurricular engagement, whether through activities or volunteer work, helps create a captivating personal resume and a portfolio of achievements that your future employers will like. Your tennis lessons might feel like simple relaxation after school, but to your future employer, they might show that you have the discipline and stamina to take over responsibilities that other applicants don't. Adding a list of skills to your resume helps make you more competitive in the workplace. Schools and colleges train students for certain occupations, but personal interests provide the individual training that forms skills that make you stand out.

Hobbies and Education Choices

Students all learn the same subjects and topics in highschool. Because of this, they finish highschool equipped with sufficient skills to start working jobs that don't require other certifications, and they have enough knowledge to become valuable members of society. But, if you wish to pursue further education, you might find yourself lost when it comes to choosing your next school and major subject. If you pursue other hobbies and interests, you will have a pretty good picture about what you want and should do as a career. Depending on how successful you were in your hobbies, you might even have some projects and achievements under your belt. Perhaps you are already in a relevant sports team or you've sold a couple of art pieces. Or, you won at a couple of singing competitions and you have plenty to show for yourself. With a background like this, it will be a lot easier to decide what to study next. Plus, you'll have an advantage over other candidates if you already have a background in the same area. Even better, you can combine your studies to choose subjects that complement one another. An already established background in design or programming, when paired with law or business studies, equips you to participate in the market without having to rely on other experts. You might mix and match expertise to learn how to make a business out of your skills successfully.

Upgrading From Extracurricular Activities to Future Opportunities

Many talented teen girls begin their careers even before they finish highschool. They might not work formally, but maybe they participate in competitions, earn rewards, or even sign contracts with sports teams, modeling agencies, or dance schools to become a permanent part of their team—for a paycheck! However, this takes a lot of devoted work on top of having the right talent and skills. You need a natural inclination for a certain activity, years of work on perfecting your skills, plus personal drive, motivation, stamina, and discipline to follow through with training and commitments. Luckily, you still have the time to find your ideal place to secure your future. All it takes is a little bit of self-reflection, testing, finding what you both love and are good at, and then investing a lot of time and hard work into doing it.

Combining Interests to Find Out What You're About

If you're good at hockey, but you'd like to become a doctor, why not go for sports medicine? If you enjoy modeling, but you want a more stable career, why not pursue business studies and/or design? Many skills complement each other to create marketable skills and businesses. For example, if you have a background in sports and become a doctor, you can access programs that would enable you to start your own clinic that works specifically with athletes. Or, if you have a background in art, but you're also interested in psychology, you can gear academic studies toward art therapy—helping people get better mentally using creativity. This would require some exploration alongside your parents, but could potentially result in many exciting, yet lucrative future opportunities.

Chapter 10:

Overcome Fears and Anxieties

What Is Anxiety?

More and more teenagers experience anxiety. For some, it's a feeling of concern, nervousness, general doubt that things will go well, or fearing negative outcomes. The more we talk about anxiety, the more it becomes obvious that almost everyone has it. In fact, most people experience anxiety several times in their lives. As you'll learn, anxiety isn't an illness that makes you different from everyone else. It won't keep you from living a fulfilled life, if you learn how to manage it. In this chapter, we'll talk about how to manage anxiety as a teenager and what to do to regain inner peace and calm.

Meaning

Whenever you experience overwhelming fear, worry, and unease, it means that you're anxious. However, there are several types and levels of severity that determine whether you're just temporarily anxious or your anxiety is getting out of hand. For example, it's normal to feel anxious before a test, while waiting for your date to show up, or before an interview. However, if this sense of unease begins to color your mood and intervene with normal, daily life, it means that you should get help. The common symptoms of anxiety are feeling restless, being unable to fall asleep or struggling with it, feeling your heart beat strongly, or feeling like you struggle to breathe.

What Does It Look and Feel Like to Be Anxious?

Everyone experiences anxiety in different ways. Some girls just feel like they're nervous all the time, while others feel moody and struggle with situations like public performances and speech. If you have anxiety, thoughts might be racing through your head all the time, to the point where you're unable to calm down. Sometimes, you might worry about something bad happening to you or someone you love. You also might have nightmares, become afraid of being alone, experience an increase of appetite, and avoid being around close friends and family members.

What Causes Anxiety

There's no single cause of anxiety. Therapists and psychologists agree, based on their personal experience and research, that some people have more tendency to worry than others. There are genetic factors that make it harder for people to regulate their mood, and there are also genetic factors that affect brain functioning. These factors can make someone more prone to negative moods. People with tendencies like these have difficulty recovering from negative feelings, and parts of their brain in charge of fear and the state of alertness are more active compared to others. Also, brain chemicals that serve to regulate mood might work differently in some people than they do with others. However, experiences and how you were taught to think about life also plays a hand in how much anxiousness you'll have throughout life.

Myths About Anxiety: It's Not ALL Bad

Anxiety is a frequent topic with most students I work with. It appears that most, if not all, teenagers struggle with it one way or another. Some only temporarily, before tests and important events, and others more frequently, like when they worry about their family, future, risks that surround us, etc. For some students, anxiety becomes so severe that they need a therapist, and sometimes, medications. I believe that the reason why so many young girls and boys have anxiety is being exposed to too many expectations while simultaneously witnessing so much negativity all around.

Fake images of perfection that come from social media make you think that most girls have an effortlessly amazing life. They wake up looking amazing, always have everything they need, and seem to cope with social difficulties with so much grace compared to regular people. At the same time, you read about all the tragedies and disasters that happen all around the world while facing personal difficulties of your own at the same time. All of this, combined, can create many different conflicts. On one hand, you might feel like happiness and having everything you want should come effortlessly, as it appears to come to so many girls. But, on the other hand, being surrounded by social negativity can make you feel like perfection is unavailable to you, personally, because of some of your flaws and limitations. Although all of this is wrong, it is real. More than trying to simply stop being anxious, you can try to make good things happen and start to reframe your worries.

Of course, you should get therapy if you feel like your symptoms are too severe. If you're upset throughout the majority of the day, regardless of what's going on in your life, get help. The same goes if you struggle with sleep and eating, and if your nervousness is affecting your social life and grades. However, there are some good sides of anxiety that are worth noting.

For example, I met students who are so anxious that they can barely give a presentation and others that are even more anxious but see themselves in a better light. They compliment themselves on being so hard-working that they stayed up until two in the morning studying and prepared for their presentation by rehearsing in front of their friends. There, I realized that not everyone benefits from looking at anxiety as this bad, negative thing. Although you should address your tendency to worry, you shouldn't look at yourself as someone who is damaged or ill because of their anxiety. Instead, you can list how it affects your behavior, and look at some of your traits as being diligent, hard-working, responsible, and dependable.

Let me tell you a secret. After learning so much about anxiety, I start noticing that more people have it than they realize. However, many of these people are very successful and quite happy. They might have, consciously or unconsciously, learned to cope with it in all the right ways. For example, I have a coworker who thinks of herself as "overly dramatic," as she describes. She is able to tell that she makes a huge deal of certain things, like preparing reports and giving presentations, but she's also able to joke about it, and she doesn't let that stop her from living an amazing life. She is just one of many, of course, and not everyone has this ability to reframe anxiety. But, you can start to think about certain ways in which your natural tendencies benefit you, and you can, indeed, decide to keep them.

How to Cope With Anxiety

As I mentioned earlier, not everyone with anxiety lets it control their life. It is possible to overcome it, but not in a typical way in which people heal from health problems. You can't exactly follow a prescribed course of treatment and heal after a certain number of days. Instead, you can learn how to calm yourself and stop racing thoughts from overwhelming. For this, you first need to learn how to calm down, reduce and ignore intrusive (sudden and scary) thoughts, and let them go so that you can focus more on the present. There are a couple of things that you need to do learn how to do first:

How to Calm a Racing Mind

When you're experiencing anxiety, it almost feels like a brain flare-up. Your mind is consumed by racing thoughts, many of which don't have anything to do with the current situation. What do you do? The only way to reduce these symptoms is to learn how to calm yourself. A lot of the time, people of all ages feel like they need to think their way through a state or a situation when they don't have to. With anxiety, the actual solution is to shift focus away from thoughts. Let me tell you a little secret: Everyone thinks all sorts of outrageous things all the time. But, most people are unaware of these thoughts because they're not upset. The more attention is given to racing thoughts, the worse they become. Since it's impossible to stop thinking, the best thing you can do to "get out of your head" is use these exercises:

- **Take three deep breaths.** Using the "rule of threes" as I like to call it, take three deep belly breaths, each taking three seconds to breathe in, pause, and breathe out.
- **Move and focus on your body.** Take a couple of steps across the room, or if you're sitting, move your legs around.
- **Focus on the present.** Look around and scan the entire room. Then, pay attention to what you're doing, and engage in an activity.

Intrusive Thoughts: What Are They and How Not to Take Them Seriously

These overwhelming, racing thoughts are also called "intrusive thoughts," and they're typical for anxiety and depression. With anxiety, these thoughts concern insecurities, doubts, conflicts, and often have disturbing content. If you ever tried to get yourself through reading your essay out loud, in front of the entire class, and found yourself thinking something outrageous about the teacher or a classmate, there's nothing wrong with you. Thoughts like these happen as a response to stress and don't have an exact explanation. Since the content of thoughts can be really disturbing, they can make you question what kind of a person you are or even doubt your sanity. Typically, intrusive thoughts worsen with growing anxiety and reduce as you calm down.

With anxiety, you constantly feel like you're in some sort of emergency, so your mind does it's best to remind you that it isn't safe to calm down. For example, you might be stroking your pet when you suddenly see an image in your mind of them being hit by a car. This is your brain's way of telling you, "The world is a terrible, dangerous place. You can't relax and enjoy it or else something bad will happen." To overcome anxiety, you must learn how to ignore these thoughts—no matter how scary and disturbing they become.

There aren't exact steps for dealing with intrusive thoughts. You simply need to develop a habit of doing the exact opposite of what the thoughts tell you. In the previous example, instead of fearing for your pet's life, snuggle with them even more and assure yourself that both of you are ok. Avoid giving attention to intrusive thoughts or else they'll become even more frequent and intense. Remember, no matter how inappropriate or violent these thoughts are, they have nothing to do with who you are as a person.

How to "Live in the Present Moment"

The final piece of the solving-anxiety puzzle is learning how to ignore all the negativity in your mind and simply choose to live a positive, satisfying life. Many people fall into a trap of trying to think their way into positivity, which doesn't work. You might think that you have to start having a positive mindset before you're able to be happy, but that's not true. It's the action that matters, and it's the action that changes how you think and feel—not the way around.

If you think about what negativity makes you do, you quickly see that it makes you self-destructive. It drives you away from friends and family, keeps you from studying, prevents you from getting exercise, and pretty much keeps you from doing anything good for yourself and others. What does this tell you? If you wish to overcome anxiety, you first need to start doing different things, which then gives you a different story to tell yourself and change how you feel.

How to Reduce Anxiety

Now that you know that the best way to reduce anxiety isn't to change your thoughts, but actions, let's discuss the simplest things that you can do for that:

Reduce Tech and Screen Time

Technology and screens trigger stress. Even if you choose to filter out all content that reaches you through social media, it's impossible to escape negativity. While technology is a useful tool when used carefully, screens emit lighting that's not healthy for your eyes, brain, and biorhythm. More and more young children these days have damaged focus abilities and eyesight from too much screen time, and the same goes for teenagers. Screens link to anxiety because they alter your brain activity. Being in front of a screen excites the brain, which isn't good unless there's a real reason to be excited about. Strong colors, light flashes, not to mention intense and violent content that always finds its way to your computer, all teach your brain that it constantly needs to be in an alert state. It's not the same as reading a book or discussing your assignment outside with a friend and writing down notes. The longer this lasts, the more your brain is in an excited state when it shouldn't be. This increases your sensitivity to fear and makes it harder to calm down and come back from difficult experiences. Finally, too much screen time in the evening directly causes problems with sleeping. Not getting enough sleep further worsens anxiety.

Go to Bed Early—You're Not Missing Out!

Sleep avoidance is typical for anxiety. Not only does your racing mind refuse to calm down, but it also doesn't feel like it's safe to relax. This leads to so-called sleep avoidance, or "sleep procrastination." To overcome this, go to bed earlier and avoid doing major activities after dinner. Your brain needs time to calm down, so try to reduce evening activities whenever possible.

Eat Well for a Calm Mind

There are several ways in which food affects anxiety:

- What do you eat? Fast food leads to immune flare-ups inside your body, and directly affects your mood. They have too much fat, sugar, and salt. Inside the body, these chemicals harm your intestines and cause bacteria and viruses to penetrate your blood and brain. When this happens, your body activates the immune system to keep major infections from happening. But, all of this causes a bad mood and nervousness. When you eat healthy foods, as I already mentioned, these immune reactions decrease, and your brain is able to start producing beneficial chemicals that make you feel calm and collected.

- When do you eat? Avoid eating a lot in the late evening. This upsets the stomach and makes it difficult to sleep well. It also elevates your blood sugar and makes you feel sluggish in the morning. Feeling slow, tired, and sluggish is known to worsen anxiety. Eat a filling breakfast, lunch, and early dinner. Don't snack too much afterward, but if you must, eat only a small piece of fruit.

- How do you eat? People who have anxiety tend to eat too fast. Often, they eat larger quantities of food too quickly, in a rush, or in front of the TV. This makes a person feel even more nervous. Instead, take at least 30 minutes for each meal. Eat slowly and chew each bite until you've felt its flavor. Doing this helps your stomach digest slowly, creating less gas and heartburn. Eating slowly will prevent feeling heavy and tired after a meal, which will reduce anxiety symptoms.

Journal and Confront Insecurities

The final change in your behavior concerns how you act in life. The change needed to stop feeling so worried comes in two major steps:

- Journaling about fears and insecurities: Each day, write down thoughts that scare and bug you. They might be about social life and how others see you, or they might be about school. Perhaps, you're afraid of public speaking, what someone in class thought about something you said yesterday, or if anyone noticed that you had a stain on your pants yesterday. After writing down all of these thoughts, figure out what to do to test or challenge them. The majority of stressful thoughts make you want to shy away. Do the opposite instead. Plan for how to interact more with people who make you feel insecure and how to do more of the things that scare you, like raising your hand to speak your mind, reading your essay out loud, or asking your crush out.

- Confronting fears in a safe, appropriate manner: To overcome anxiety, it's ideal to do the things that scare you and show yourself that you're able to cope with the experience. However, this should be done in an appropriate, safe way. You can choose to talk more to people or approach those girls who make you feel insecure or unworthy. Or, you might write out a scenario for what you'll say or do if someone teases and provokes you. Doing this over and over again shows your brain that there's nothing to worry about and that you're capable of keeping yourself safe and going through challenging situations.

Chapter 11

Girl Stuff: Just Between Us!

Joys and Hardships of Dating

Up until recently, you might have had one or two crushes. Someone caught your attention, whether because of their looks or their personality. You used to enjoy becoming a bit closer as friends with this person, at least temporarily. But now, this no longer feels like enough. Whether you're 15, 16, or 17, your teen years typically mark your first date. However, dating can become a source of all sorts of hardship for teenage girls. Deciding whether to accept an invitation from a boy, breaking the news to your parents, and even deciding if you're ready is a major journey. Before you start, remember to talk to your parents, confide in them, and make decisions together.

Are You Ready to Date?

Dating isn't only a matter of liking each other and having a good time. It's a sensitive thing both for you and the other person. What now looks like a simple dinner and movie might turn into a lot of confusion and misunderstanding if you haven't taken everything into account. First, dating is an emotional experience. You should let your parents know that you're interested in going on a date and make sure to have their permission before accepting the invitation. Talk to them about how you feel about the other person, and how they treat you and make you feel. Before going on a date, talk to your parents about setting boundaries for where to go, what to do, and whether or not to kiss or get in other physical contact. This might sound strange, but clearing all this up beforehand will help you feel like you know what you're doing and can help you relax and enjoy your date more.

Who to Pick: Find Out What You Value

You have the right and the duty to make the best picks for yourself. Some girls get more attention from boys than others, but don't worry about this! You shouldn't feel like you have to accept anyone just because they've expressed an interest in you or like you have to settle for someone who you don't like just because you don't get asked out often. No matter the circumstances, you have the right to set standards for yourself regarding the qualities that you want your date to have. Think about character traits, style, manners, likes, dislikes, preferences, and beliefs. If you and your family have strong moral, social, or religious beliefs and philosophies, it's important for your match to fit into that concept as well.

Rejection: How to Accept It Gracefully and Recover

Asking a boy out and getting rejected hurts. But, so does getting hurt from a girl who they asked out. If you ask a boy out, and they say "no," it's not a big deal! This means that he doesn't feel the same way about you, and that's OK. It doesn't mean that you've embarrassed yourself or that there's something wrong with you. It also doesn't mean that you should give up on asking boys out. However, if you felt like there was a chance that your crush liked you, but they didn't, it's possible that you misunderstood some of their words or actions. Think about the 'signals' that you thought meant that they were romantically interested when they weren't. In the future, when another boy does similar things, remember that it doesn't necessarily have to be romantic, and take that into account when deciding whether to ask them out.

Stay Safe: How to Protect Yourself

Whether you've gotten asked out, or your crush accepted your invitation, it's important to keep safety in mind. No matter how well you two know each other, you shouldn't visit unsafe locations, drink alcohol, or hang out with strange people who you don't know. Make sure that your crush introduces themselves to your parents. Let your parents know the exact location of your date and don't change what's been agreed.

Understand Boys

Are they from Mars? Were they sent to Earth just to bug us, or what? Depending on how you get along with boys, you might find them to be the same type of human as yourself, or you might think of them as childish and annoying. When boys become special to you, it gets that much more confusing. You're likely confused about how you feel, plus about how he feels, and whether or not things he says and does and the way he does it means that he feels the same way about you. I know, it's a hussle! Could dating be more complicated? Indeed, teenage dating is the most stressful and confusing stage of a person's romantic life, and it gets easier with time and experience.

What Boys and Girls Have in Common

Beneath the surface, boys and girls have the same needs, similar thoughts and aspirations, goals, likes, and dislikes. Teenage boys are most, if not all of the time, quite insecure about their appearance, social competence, and what others think about them. They want to be accepted and loved, seen and appreciated for the person they are, and to do the best they can with what they know. This is important to remember, since at your age, how a person looks, dresses, behaves, does at school and socially isn't always a sole reflection of their personality. The same way like yourself, boys your age are sensitive to what goes on at their home, and that can affect how they speak and act.

The way they dress often reflects their family's financial well-being, and not necessarily their personal style and preference.

What Makes Boys Different Than Girls

While both boys and girls face the same struggles with puberty and growing up, they are biologically different—and so are the changes. Boys have similar mood changes as girls, but they're more likely to get angry and frustrated thanks to changing hormones. Boys also tend to act differently around their friends than they do with girlfriends, and that's normal. However, sometimes, they can go overboard with teasing, either to show off or to cope with shyness. In that case, you should let him know that you won't put up with mistreatment. However, keep in mind that a lot of their silly behaviors are just a way for them to cope with shyness. Although no one likes to be shy, it's better accepted for girls than it is for boys. Your friends might understand that you feel awkward in certain situations, but his friends may not.

How to Have Healthy, Genuine, and Honest Relationships

Adolescence is a time when boys and girls learn about relationships. Conversations aimed at decoding the secret language of relationships boil down to "What did it mean when he said [X] or [Y]?" or "Will he say/do [X] or [Y] if I say/wear/do [X] or [Y]?" How about choosing a new way to communicate? Both of you have insecurities, and are, in many ways, afraid of one another. That's OK, and it will go away with age. Honesty and communicating what you think and how you feel helps prevent lies, misunderstandings, and conflict. It's also important to discuss issues with your date/boyfriend first before sharing any stories with your friends.

Puberty

What's going on with your body? Why is it starting to look different each day? Why are you feeling so moody and tired all of a sudden? Why do you get a sudden urge to move and go out, and then, out of the blue, you start craving a nap? It's called puberty, or adolescence. Hormonal changes that come with this stage of growing up, or maturation, cause both physical and mental changes.

Why Are You Suddenly Different?

Each girl experiences puberty differently. However, there are common changes that happen to your body in similar order. First, you might notice that you've developed breast buds, and your breasts continue to grow. Then, you'll notice the growth of pubic and armpit hair, as well as hair on your legs and arms. Your body shape will also change. You might grow in weight and height, particularly in arms and legs—which can make you feel awkward. As your body begins to produce hormones, you'll eventually get your first period. Periods will continue to happen every month, although it's common for them to be irregular at first.

Changes in Puberty: How Your Body and Mind Develop

Mentally, you're also growing and getting smarter. You are gaining the ability to think on an abstract level beyond what's obvious. You'll start thinking and engaging in social issues, politics, and philosophy. You are now able to set long-term goals and think about the future. You might have strong opinions about certain issues, like equality, animal rights, and environment. You also might feel emotionally hurt or angry whenever you witness injustice, that's normal. If you wish to engage in community work, I recommend looking into local organizations and charities that support the marginalized, whether it's through fundraising or charity work.

You might feel like you need more space from your parents, but that might cause friction and arguments between you. While you might want more solace and privacy, your parents might be worried about what goes on in your life. They might worry that you're in some sort of trouble or that someone is hurting you. That's why they might act suspicious of you, although you've done nothing wrong.

It's also normal to want your friends to accept you, but you shouldn't fall under the pressure of doing anything you're uncomfortable with just to get others' approval. Think about ongoing trends in your friend group and establish firm boundaries about what you want and don't want to accept.

Final Tips for Girls: Five Do's and Don'ts

Do

Respect, Cherish, and Love Yourself

Self-love and compassion are the two pillars of self-esteem, empowerment, and mental balance. They can help you overcome anxiety and gain inner peace. Prioritize self-love and respect as a role-model for how to treat others as well. They'll help you communicate and compromise in the most challenging circumstances.

Have a Healthy Relationship With Others

Teenage relationships can get toxic. You might think it's because of malice or because one person wants to hurt the other. It's not. Most of the time, it's because of misconceptions, misunderstandings, acting on assumptions, or others' personal issues. Don't let yourself get sucked into toxic relationships! Try to fix what can be fixed, but if anyone is hurting you, always talk to your parents and teachers.

Have Age-Appropriate Fun

It's great to get together with friends, go out, and share quality time together. However, you shouldn't engage in underage drinking, substance use, or sex before you've talked about it with your parents. There's a reason why all of these things are considered inappropriate for teenagers. They can cloud your judgment and impair physical and mental health.

Grow Your Authenticity

You might feel a lot of pressure to be like everyone else—to wear what everyone else wears, to get similar makeup, do the same hairstyles, go to the same places, and do what everyone else does. Only accept what you feel to be right for you, and don't be afraid of being different!

Talk to Your Parents/Caregivers

Be open about how you feel and what goes on in your life, even if it means that sometimes you'll get in an argument with your closest family members. You are changing, and they too have a difficult time coping with the loss of the child that they knew and getting to know someone new.

Don't

Try to Grow Up Too Soon

Girls who wear too much makeup and dress too flashy don't look good. The type of attention that you'll get affects your mental and emotional well-being. However, it depends on you as much as it depends on other people. Others are responsible for their words and actions, but the way you act and carry yourself sends a message about the type of person who you want to be—and people will react accordingly.

Dye Your Hair and Wear Too Much Make-up

Hair dye can cause long-term damage to your hair and scalp, while too much make up causes wrinkles and break-outs. Remember that all of these accessories serve to make a woman look younger, not older. Be happy that you still don't need them, and use only as much as to show your unique style and refresh your look.

Succumb to Peer Pressure

Sometimes, friends and classmates might put pressure on your to use substances, drink, bully, and engage in sexual activities. If this happens, remove yourself from the situation right away and call your parents or someone who can get you back home. If peer pressure is happening at school, let your teacher know. If you feel like the situation could get violent, talk to your parents to alert authorities.

Put Anyone Before School, Health, and Well-Being

Social life and romance might feel like the greatest priorities, but they're not. Don't let anyone get in the way of your health, well-being, and long-term goals. Stay focused on what truly matters in life!

Conclusion

Wow, what a journey! In *Life Coaching for Teenage Girls. A Practical Guide to Help Achieve Total Empowerment*, I wanted to help you gain the knowledge needed for independent work on your personal growth, fulfillment, and achievement—whether it's creative or academic.

You now know that the core of empowerment lies in self-esteem, and you understand what self-esteem is, and how to strengthen it. You can assume what happens when you feel insecure, like falling under people's pressure, tolerating mistreatment, or becoming aggressive. There are so many ways you've learned to rely on to recover when your self-esteem is damaged, like becoming more independent and learning about skills, talents, your positive traits, and how to accept responsibility.

Second, you read about what social skills are and why they're important—to make friends, network, and get opportunities in real life. You're able to form essential social skills for friendships, and more importantly, you know how to gain them through experience, exercise, authenticity, and showing your true self. We discussed the need to "read the room," or try to understand the situation that you're in to decide what's best to say and do. Aside from this, it's important to listen to others and show concern but to also express yourself and contribute your unique insight to any discussion. A great part of having good social skills is to learn how to accept rejection, which can be done gracefully and with dignity.

Third, success requires organization. You now understand what organization is and how to designate time and plan for all of your tasks, belongings, and items. You can reap the many benefits of planning and knowing what your general and specific goals are. Rely on the process of achieving goals, which starts with planning milestones and tasks, and then do your best to overcome obstacles that arise. You can do this with timely preparation and making sure that your plans are realistic.

Fourth, you know about mindfulness and its potential to help you get healthier and happier. You can practice mindfulness with art and exercises like breathing, meditation, walks, and focus. There are a couple of things to be cautious with when it comes to practicing mindfulness, like manipulation, escapism, and overthinking. You understand that mindfulness has a lot to do with motivation or the driving force behind all of the amazing things that you're doing. There are certain things that can diminish your motivation, like hardship, trauma, and insecurity, but you can also bring it back up with the right, balanced lifestyle—discovering what values, goals, and visions drive you—and timely planning and preparations. You can regain your ability to focus and prevent your concentration from being compromised. In order to regain the ability to concentrate, you need to first declutter your mind and then persist through hardship by being aware of your motives, goals, and purpose.

Fifth, you embraced the ability to empower yourself and find inner strength. We covered what personal power is and what numerous strengths you can tap into to harvest that power. You can empower yourself by being critical, standing up for yourself and others, and learning how to set and accept boundaries. You've gained insight into how important it is to have a positive mindset in life. Positivity and resilience come from the ability to reframe negative experiences and thoughts using self-love and compassion. You also read about how important it is to channel negative feelings into something productive, like arts, crafts, and movement. Media affects how you think and feel, which is why it's necessary to pay closer attention to the content that you consume.

Finally, you were introduced to many ways to explore your talents, interests, and skills. You can use hobbies to not only spend quality time outside school and have fun but also to learn about your talents and skills for future opportunities and career planning. Plus, you are empowered to deal with anxiety, let go of negative thoughts, and change your behaviors to transform your mindset and see better outcomes in real life. Ultimately, doing all of the things that were recommended in this book will help you get better grades, have closer friendships and relationships, and feel physically and mentally well. Remember to nurture your authenticity, take care of yourself first, and respect yourself the same way you cherish and appreciate those you love the most!

Author Bio

Justine Cousins, the author of *Life Coaching for Teenage Girls: A Practical Guide to Help Achieve Total Empowerment*, is a mother of three teenage girls and a passionate enthusiast for self-help and personal growth.

Her journey in learning about self-help and personal development began upon the birth of her first daughter. Justine learned the importance of living toward the completion of goals. Goals, in the beginning, were to be a good role model for her daughters and to provide the empowerment needed for a girl to become strong, independent, and to feel well-integrated into a supportive environment.

Throughout the years of bringing up her children, Justine realized that there was a gap between the knowledge she learned from self-help books and her real-life experience. Something wasn't adding up, and, in her mind, it was the lack of acknowledgment for each girl's individual experience.

With this in mind, Justine devoted her life to not only learning about empowering teenage girls and guiding them toward achievement but also providing the sort of uplifting, joyous take on life's hurdles that each girl needed to thrive and live her best life. From there, she tested every bit of information and took feedback from teenagers she knew well. The result of her work was a curious collision of science with the sardoodledom of adolescence.

References

11 Facts about teens and self esteem. (2015). DoSomething.org. https://www.dosomething.org/us/facts/11-facts-about-teens-and-self-esteem

50 Social skills for teens. (2018, March 22). Learning For a Purpose. https://learningforapurpose.com/2018/03/22/50-social-skills-for-teens/

biglifejournal.com. (n.d.). *15 Tips to build self esteem and confidence in teens.* Big Life Journal. https://biglifejournal.com/blogs/blog/build-self-esteem-confidence-teens

Bluth, K. (2016, March 23). *Five tips for teaching mindfulness to at-risk teens.* Greater Good. https://greatergood.berkeley.edu/article/item/five_tips_for_te aching_mindfulness_to_at_risk_teens

Eckert, M., Ebert, D. D., Lehr, D., Sieland, B., & Berking, M. (2016). Overcome procrastination: Enhancing emotion regulation skills reduce procrastination. *Learning and Individual Differences, 52,* 10–18. https://doi.org/10.1016/j.lindif.2016.10.001

Eva, A. L. (2018, May 21). *Five ways to help teens feel good about themselves.* Greater Good. https://greatergood.berkeley.edu/article/item/five_ways_to_h elp_teens_feel_good_about_themselves

Happiness and wellbeing for teenagers. (n.d.). Raising Children Network. https://raisingchildren.net.au/teens/mental-health-physical-health/about-mental-health/happy-teens

Kim, Y., & Campano, L. (2021, December 15). *How to tell your crush you like them without making things weird.* Seventeen.

https://www.seventeen.com/love/dating-advice/a26324989/how-to-tell-someone-you-like-them/

Li, A. P., MS, & MBA. (2021, March 13). *How to motivate teenager to study using Brain science.* Parenting for Brain. https://www.parentingforbrain.com/how-to-motivate-teenager-to-study/

Mindfulness for teens. (2014, December 31). Mindfulness for Teens. http://mindfulnessforteens.com/

Mindfulness for teens: The benefits of meditation in a busy world. (n.d.). Www.georgetownbehavioral.com. https://www.georgetownbehavioral.com/blog/mindfulness-for-teens

Monroe, J. (2017, April 5). *Positive thinking for teens.* Newport Academy. https://www.newportacademy.com/resources/mental-health/positivity-teen-mental-health/

Morin, A. (n.d.). *How to teach your high-schooler organization skills.* www.understood.org. https://www.understood.org/articles/en/at-a-glance-7-ways-to-teach-your-high-schooler-organization-skills

Morin, A. (2021, February 20). *How parents can help their teen build self-confidence.* Verywell Family. https://www.verywellfamily.com/essential-strategies-for-raising-a-confident-teen-2611002

Nelsen, J., & Lott, L. (2016, May 5). *How do you motivate a teen? Yes, it is possible!* positivediscipline.com. https://www.positivediscipline.com/articles/how-do-you-motivate-teen-yes-it-possible

Panlilio, D. (2021, December 17). *How to encourage a teenager to take up a hobby.* WikiHow. https://www.wikihow.com/Encourage-a-Teenager-to-Take-Up-a-Hobby

Pickhardt, C. E. (2013, June 24). *Adolescents, parents, and the management of personal power.* Psychology Today.

https://www.psychologytoday.com/us/blog/surviving-your-childs-adolescence/201306/adolescents-parents-and-the-management-personal-power

Price, A. (2018, April 17). *4 Reasons why teens can't stop procrastinating*. Psychology Today. https://www.psychologytoday.com/us/blog/the-unmotivated-teen/201804/4-reasons-why-teens-cant-stop-procrastinating

Psychology, T. B. B. (n.d.). *Teen dating advice*. LoveToKnow. Retrieved January 2, 2022, from https://dating.lovetoknow.com/Teen_Dating

Raising Healthy Teens. (2019, December 31). *Tips to help your teen cultivate their passion*. Raising Healthy Teens Orange County. https://raisinghealthyteens.org/rht_blog/tips-to-help-your-teen-cultivate-their-passion/

Reach Out. (2019). *Self-esteem and teenagers*. Reachout.com. https://parents.au.reachout.com/common-concerns/everyday-issues/self-esteem-and-teenagers

Reyes, M. G. (2017, November 6). *6 Ways to empower your teen daughter*. NTUC Income. https://www.income.com.sg/blog/empower-your-teen-daughter

Robson, D. (n.d.). *The best social skills activities and resources for teens*. And Next Comes L. https://www.andnextcomesl.com/2020/07/social-skills-activities-for-teens.html

Shipman, C., Kay, K., & Riley, J. (2018, October 1). The confidence gap for girls: 5 tips for parents of tween and teen girls. *The New York Times*. https://www.nytimes.com/2018/10/01/well/family/confidence-gap-teen-girls-tips-parents.html

Simeon, D. (2014, March 6). *Want your teen to be more organized? 10 ideas that actually work*. Your Teen Magazine.

https://yourteenmag.com/teenager-school/teenager-middle-school/help-your-teenager-get-organized

Sugarman, L. (2019, February 21). *A mom's practical dating advice for teenage girls*. Grown and Flown. https://grownandflown.com/moms-practical-dating-advice-for-teenage-girls/

The 7 secrets of motivating teenagers. (2012, September 17). Understanding Teenagers. https://understandingteenagers.com.au/the-7-secrets-of-motivating-teenagers/

Townsend, J. (2017, May 19). *Helping your teen gain healthy personal power*. Compass Rose Academy. https://compassroseacademy.org/helping-teen-gain-healthy-personal-power/

Understood Team. (n.d.-a). *6 Ways to help your child focus*. www.understood.org. https://www.understood.org/articles/en/how-to-improve-focus-in-kids

Understood Team. (n.d.-b). *Tools and tips to help your teen get organized*. www.understood.org. https://www.understood.org/articles/en/tools-and-tips-to-help-your-teen-get-organized

Verma, P. (2019, January 6). *Destroy negativity from your mind with this simple exercise*. Medium. https://medium.com/the-mission/a-practical-hack-to-combat-negative-thoughts-in-2-minutes-or-less-cc3d1bddb3af